bro-
stuart's

guide to
living cheaply in
SAN FRANCISCO

Falls Media

Merry Christmas 2008
Love,
Nick

Published by Falls Media
565 Park Avenue, Suite 11E
New York, NY 10021

First Printing, November 2007
10 9 8 7 6 5 4 3 2

Design by Mike Force
Cover Design by Kenny Liu
Maps by Angela Hathaway

ISBN-13 978-0-9788178-9-3

"You look back and see how hard you worked and how poor you were, and how desperately anxious you were to succeed, and all you can remember is how happy you were."

~ Jack London

"You are Young, Broke, and Beautiful."

~ Broke-Ass Stuart

YOU ARE YOUNG, BROKE, AND BEAUTIFUL.

brokeassstuart.com

Table of Contents

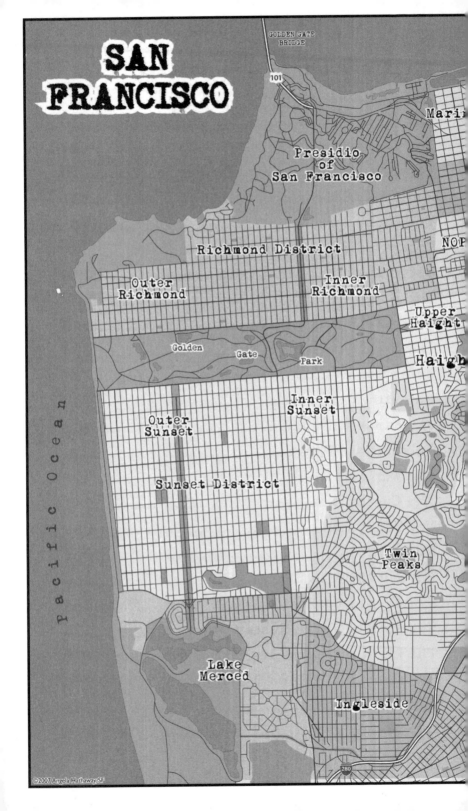

MUNI Metro and BART Transit

©2007 Angela Hathaway, SF

Jefferson & Jones

Pier 39

Embarcadero & Chestnut

Embarcadero & Union

Embarcadero

Montgomery

to East Bay

N

16th St & Mission

Church & 18th St

Castro

Church & 24th St

24th St & Mission

urch & 0th St

an Jose & Randall

Glen Park

LEGEND

N Judah

J Church

L Taraval

M Oceanview

K Ingleside

F Market
(Stops almost every block on Market)

BART (Bay Area Rapid Transit)

MUNI Surface Stop*

MUNI Underground Station

BART Station

*Not all MUNI surface stops are shown, just main stops and handicapped accessible stops. Complete MUNI transit maps can be found in the underground stations, at MUNI bus shelters, or at www.sfmuni.com

Introduction

I have absolutely the biggest crush on San Francisco. I mean seriously, have you ever met someone who's been to this city and said, "Nah man, fuck San Francisco. I can't stand that place"? Me neither. Sure, I've got friends who say they could never live here, but they still love it and can't wait to come back and sleep on my couch again. Why is that? I think in part it's because, as far as cities go, this one is beautiful. It's got hills, lots of green parks, water on three sides, famous architecture and of course, cute little cable cars. And yeah, sure, we all know San Francisco is an epicenter for all things concerning good food and good wine.

But really, all those things are peripheral in the grand scheme of things. What makes this city so fucking great is that everybody here has a little bit of freak and weirdo in them. Just look at Bay to Breakers, where tens of thousands of people either dress up in costumes or get naked and push shopping carts full of beer for miles across the City.

If U.S. cities were people, San Francisco would be the weird art

When Emperor Norton (see the Eye Spy Game on page 164) first proposed building a bridge to Oakland in the 1870's, people thought he was crazy (which he was).

school kid who felt like nobody else understood him. Whether you live in the Mission or the Marina, there's a reason why you chose San Francisco—you chose it because there was something about this city that spoke to you and made you feel like this was home. And you know what that means? You're just as loony as the rest of us, whether you like it or not.

Everybody knows somebody in San Francisco, which means that whether you're visiting from Australia or living in the Sunset, there's always a chance that you're gonna bump into someone you know. So just remember that San Francisco is a city where you can't escape your past. Not that that's a bad thing. I love it when I walk down Haight Street and bump into someone I met in Venice when I was 20. One of the great things about this City is that everyone seems to know each other, or they are separated by fewer than three degrees, making SF feel even more like a community.

Fuck, I guess what I'm trying to say through all this babbling is that there is so much to love about this City, and either you love it as much as I do, or you want to know more about it, so you can fall in love with it. I mean why else would you have bought this book? Oh yeah, because you're just as brok~ ~~ ~

Who the Fuck is Broke-Ass Stuart?

I was working in a candy store in North Beach when all this madness started. A guy from my neighborhood growing up, who was a few years older than me, came into the store with his wife-to-be (I'm assuming they're married by now). It had been years since I'd seen him, so it was nice to hear what was going on in his life. After we chatted for a bit, and they bought some candy (I slang candy like a motherfucker), the fiancé handed me her card and told me that I should give them a shout next time I was in San Diego. After they left, I looked at her card, and it said she was a travel writer. I thought to myself, "Travel writer? I wanna be a travel writer," and it was then that I decided to be one.

San Francisco is a town full of cheap places to eat and drink, so when it occurred to me to write *Broke-Ass Stuart's Guide to Living Cheaply in San Francisco*, I had already built up a nice retinue of fine establishments (meaning dive bars and greasy spoon diners) from which I could draw inspiration. I was pretty fucking broke at the time (still am), and so was everyone else I knew, so

I figured I would put something together to help out all the other young struggling folks in the City. The original *Broke-Ass Stuart's* was a 33-page zine, with the only photo being the cover shot. taken in the basement .. ..

.... Bay issue. Truthfully, my reaction to this minor success was, "Holy shit! I can't believe people really dig this stuff."

By the time *Broke-Ass Stuart's Guide to Living Cheaply v.2* came out in July 2005, this shit had gotten a lot of hype. So I threw a big release party with bands, DJs, free food and a whole bunch of other crap. *Broke-Ass v.2* is when everything really took off; I sold 300 copies of it in the first week (remember this is with no PR, and I was doing all the distribution by foot and mass transit). Lots of good things came about because of it; I was on TV a few times, on the radio, got "Best of the Bay" again, people recognized me at bars, I had some groupies, and ultimately, I got to write for Lonely Planet (I did the Ireland chapter for the *Western Europe* and *Europe on a Shoestring* books). I was finally, officially, a travel writer; I even had business cards that said so.

After Ireland I decided that doing everything myself was too much work, and that if I was gonna continue to do the whole *Broke-Ass Stuart* thing, I wanted to have a publisher so all I would have to do is write books, and let them handle the rest. I blew every guy in Hollywood before I realized that the publishing industry was based in New York. Then (this part is actually real) I found Falls Media on craigslist, and conned them into putting out my books ... suckers. So here we are; I'm glad that this book has found its way to you. I don't want to say that it is fate, because I don't believe in that shit, but you and I have both made the decisions that have landed this book in your hands at this particular point in history. And so for that, I just want to say, I love you, motherfucker. I hope you enjoy reading this book as much as I enjoyed researching and writing it.

Broke-Ass Stuart

If you saw what kind of fucked up shit was going on at the front of the bus, you'd be looking out the window too. Photo by Krista Vendetti

The Mission

I f it feels like there is something going on in the Mission, that's because there is. There are so many more cool, cheap things in the Mission than in other parts of San Francisco, that it makes sense that this section is the biggest one. I lived in this neighborhood for years, so it will always have a place in my heart. The Mission is a strange mixture of Latino families and young hipsters, making it one of the more culturally diverse and interesting parts of the City. It has a stellar nightlife and is also one of the largest neighborhoods in San Francisco. Some areas can be a little shady at night, but overall it is a great neighborhood. The Mission houses some of the cheapest bars and restaurants in San Francisco and is home to the City's most politically progressive people.

There are really two main commercial drags in the Mission: Valencia Street and Mission Street. Valencia is lined with book stores, clothing boutiques, coffee shops, bars and restaurants, all of which are more geared to the Mission's young hip population.

Mission Street is lined with businesses of a very similar nature, but is instead geared towards the Latino families of the neighborhood. Of course, neither street is exclusive and there is plenty of crossover. If you are looking for a good deal, then Mission Street is your best bet because there are a lot of stores where price can be negotiated. But be prepared to use some of what you learned in tenth-grade Spanish because there are many people there who are relatively recent immigrants to the U.S. It might also help to know some Chinese or Tagalog as well.

Food

..... Thursday through
____ nights, and all the lovely tattooed/pierced/bicycle-riding hipsters you can stomach. An added bonus is that the café subscribes to a bunch of good magazines and has them on display for you to read. Atlas is also the place where a beautiful Brazilian woman once conned me into writing a five-page paper for her about Allen Ginsburg's *Howl.* Hey, don't laugh asshole! I'm not usually a chump like that, but when she invited me back to her place to help her study, I thought she meant "help her study". You would've done the same thing ... aw, fuck off, I don't have to explain myself to you.

Big Mouth Burgers
3392 24th St. @ Valencia St.

A friend of mine, who works as a cook at a nice restaurant on Pier 39, once told me that a hamburger at his restaurant cost $16. My immediate reaction was, "*Sixteen dollars!* You better at least get a reach-around with your $16 hamburger!" After I explained in Spanish what a reach-around was, he answered, "No, but it does come with some very good fries." Big Mouth Burgers also has very good fries that come with their burgers. And their burgers, while not being the cheapest in the Mission, are by no means $16. They offer a choice of burgers from hormone-free beef, to veggie, to pork loin and also let you choose between baked beans, Caesar salad or great fries. Big Mouth also proudly sells Mitchell's Ice Cream, so you can have a delicious milkshake or root beer float for dessert.

Cha Cha Cha

2327 Mission St. @ 19th St.

(see entry on page 129)

China Express

2324 Mission St. @ 24th St.

Like so many other random Chinese restaurants in the city, this place has big combo plates for pretty cheap, under $6 to be exact. It also doubles as a donut store. I can't personally vouch for this one, but hell, if you are hungry and in the area, stop in and get a donut and some wonton soup.

El Cachanilla

2948 21st St. @ Treat Ave.

If I were to guess what El Cachanilla translates to in English it would be, "not fucking around". I know that's not the translation at all, but seriously, this place makes all the other taquerias in the Mission look like total pussies. Sure I've seen other taquerias that sell tacos with *cabeza* (head fat), *tripas* (intestines), *lengua* (tongue) and even *sesos* (brains) before, but El Cachanilla one-ups them all and sells fucking *ojos* (bull eyes) too! If this were a prison movie, none of the other taquerias would mess with El Cachanilla because they'd be like, "See that guy over there? That dude is goddamn crazy. I ain't messin' with him." On a slightly more serious note though, this place does have good, cheap food ($1.50 tacos), and a little walk up taco window for if you just wanna order to go. Yo, if you do end up eating the *ojos* let me know.

El Farolito

2777 Mission St. @ 24th St.

If I'm not mistaken, El Farolito translates to "The Little Lighthouse", which is a perfect name for a place that beckons you to the safety of a big warm burrito on a dark Mission night. Open till 3 a.m. on weekends, El Farolito holds it down as one of the best tasting and cheapest burritos in the Mission. The interior is far short of spectacular, but as we always said while growing up in San Diego, the more run~~~~ ~ ~ ~

...~~ ~~~g Salvadorian food, El Trebol's prices make me feel like I'm back at home. I don't think there is a single thing on the menu more than $6.99 and most of it is actually in the $5 range. These are prices for full dishes, not just a burrito. The interior of this small restaurant is sparse yet homey, and the service is so friendly that you might feel guilty for spending your cash somewhere else.

New Yorker's Buffalo Wings
663 Valencia St. @ 18ᵗʰ St.

New Yorker's is a place you can watch a game on TV (or *Law and Order*, depending on who's got the remote) and catch a decent deal on good, greasy food. As the name suggests, their specialty is Buffalo wings and they *used to be* FAN-tastic! Although the wing quality has gone down a bit, there is almost nothing better in the world than sitting down to a bucket of 50 after marching down Valencia chanting *"Buffalo wings!"* with your friends at 2 a.m. This place is open until 3 a.m. on weekends, so now you know where to find me late at night.

Osha Thai Noodle
819 Valencia St. @19ᵗʰ St

(see entry on page 53)

Pancho Villa's
3071 16th St. @ Valencia St.

I don't know about you, but when I'm drunk as hell I crave Mexican food. I don't know why, but after a long night of boozin' it up, nothing sounds better. Since I often do my drinking in the Mission, I often end up at Pancho Villa's. This big, brightly lit place has a sort of assembly line style of putting your order together, thus making it come out efficiently, and very tasty. Henry Ford would be proud. Anyway, this place is almost as nice for your wallet as your stomach, so go there and eat damnit!

Que Tal
1005 Guerrero St. @ 22nd St.

You know how sometimes when old people say they aren't gonna do something they go, "I wouldn't do that for all the tea in China?" Well whatever that was, Que Tal did it. I've never seen such a big packaged-tea selection in my life. Other than tea drinking, this café is great for getting work done or meeting some of the cuties that live in the neighborhood.

Red Café
2894 Mission St. @ 25th St.

A great alternative to some of the Mission's more trendy breakfast spots, the Red Café is a fantastic place to have a sit down with the previous night's hangover. The food here is really good and moderately priced, the servers are all so lovely and friendly, and their corned beef hash sandwich is so good it borders on being magical. Just be warned, if wandering Mariachis have an adverse affect on your hangover, you might want to try another venue. Fortunately for me, I kinda have a thing for Mariachi music.

Revolution Café
3248 22nd St. @ Bartlett St.

Despite having a pretty ridiculous name, this is quickly becoming one of my favorite spots in the entire City. Somehow blending

European sidewalk café culture with San Francisco Mission cool-
ness, the Revolution manages to be amazingly hip and almost
completely without pretension except for the i ill

.... us u ile as naming it
the Revolution Café.

Ritual
1026 Valencia St. @ 21st St.

Simply put, Ritual makes me wish I drank coffee and/or had a
laptop. Beyond the fact that the employees make super-cool pat-
tern thingies in their lattes and shit, I wish I drank coffee just so I
didn't feel like an imposter in this place. When I go in there now
it feels like everyone knows I'm only going so I can meet pretty
girls. And the laptop thing, Jesus! I mean when you walk in everyone looks up from their iBooks in unison, gives you the once over
and then returns back to whatever they were working on—it's like
a goddamn commercial for Apple computers. The funny thing
though is that probably 80 percent of the people in Ritual are
there to pick-up/be-picked-up-on and if they tell you any differ-
ently, then they're fucking liars. That being said, everyone tells me
that Ritual's coffee is fantastic.

Serrano's Pizza
3274 21st St. @ Valencia St.

So good and well priced! They make everything, even individual
slices, to order, and their lunch specials are great. For $5.65 you
get a huge slice of cheese, a salad and a drink, and the same deal
for a cheese calzone costs $6.15. Just be careful when you get a
calzone to go because they insulate the box with tinfoil. I think I

accidentally swallowed some of the foil one time. I eat too fast and I know it's gonna be the death of me.

Smile BBQ

2619 Mission St. @ 22nd St.

Smile is a little greasy spoon of a restaurant where you can get a very good club sandwich somewhere in the mid-three dollar range. I'm horribly addicted to kiwi-strawberry Snapple, so with that added to the bill, I walk out satiated for slightly over five bucks. They also have hamburgers for under $3 and full plates of cheap BBQ as well. And to top it off, they give you a slice of gum when you pay. There's nothing like fresh breath after a good meal.

St. Francis Fountain

2801 24th St. @ York St.

It's amazing how much cool shit is in the Mission. This is an authentic soda fountain that has been around since 1918. Although the prices are not the cheapest, this place does have a candy counter where you can buy all sorts of goodies including trading cards. *Yes!!* The menu is fairly big, including such soda fountain classics as malted milkshakes, double dip sodas, and Guinness Stout in a can. The St. Francis Fountain is really a special little place that you should definitely check out.

The Tamale Lady

Wandering around dispensing goodness

This one might be a little misleading because, you don't find The Tamale Lady, she finds you. On any given night in the Mission, Virginia, aka The Tamale Lady, cruises around the bars selling her freshly made tamales, and they are friggin' amazing! She sells at least three or four different kinds and gives you hot sauce options too. And if that weren't enough, she's had the foresight to commodify herself: she sells Tamale Lady shirts and stickers. She's the Jay-Z of the Tamale game. Really, she's got mad street cred. When I had the release party for the second version of the *Broke-Ass Stuart* zine, I invited Virginia to come, hang out, and sell tamales. When people

Me and the famous Tamale Lady. By the looks of it in this photo, I've been eating a few too many tamales. Damn Stu, you lookin' thick!

advice in a bar full of drunken derelicts. So if you're out in the Mission and you're hungry or dying to get something off your chest, keep your eyes peeled, because The Tamale Lady always shows up when you least expect her. Goddamn, I love you Virginia!

Tartine

600 Guerrero St. @ 18th St.

The first time I went to this mouth-watering French-ish bakery was a funny experience. A friend of mine and her employer/benefactor were up from Los Angeles for a couple days and they took me to Tartine because they knew how amazing it was. The benefactor was giving me all this LA jive about, "Oh you've really got something here with this Broke-Ass Stuart thing. I'm gonna give a copy to my literary agent. I think you could be really big." I knew it was LA jive from the beginning and politely told him so, but figured, "What the fuck? The man bought me lunch, why not go along with it and see what happens." We had a fantastic lunch and some nice conversation, and by the end I almost believed I'd be able to get some type of book deal. Since then, I've been back to Tartine a trillion times; mostly for their bread pudding, which is so amazing that it could probably kill a truckload of diabetics, but I still haven't heard from anyone's literary agent.

Tortas El Primo
2499 Folsom St. @ 21st St.

I had to ask what the name of this spot was because the yellow awning only says things like, "Frutas, verdures, Hot Dogs, Tortas" etc. But the tortas (Mexican grilled sandwiches) here are inexpensive and gigantic. Nothing here is more than six bucks and the torta ladies don't skimp on anything. Ask for avocado and you get like half an avocado on your sandwich … awesometown!

Tortilla Flats
2000 Bryant St. @ 21st St.

You bought this book because you wanna know about cheap places to eat in the City, right? Well here you go. There's nothing over $6.50 at this basic breakfast/lunch/deli dealy, and I'm pretty sure you can get a sandwich and fries for around five bucks. The food is hit or miss (mostly miss) but there are occasionally shining moments. Just don't expect much in the way of atmosphere because, well, that's not what you're here for, is it?

WeBe Sushi
538 Valencia St. @ 16th St.;
also 1071 Valencia @ 21st St.

WeBe provides an important service in the Mission: decent tasting, cheap sushi. Somebody had to do it, and the good people of WeBe stepped up to the godforsaken plate. Your best bet is to hit them up for their lunch or dinner specials where you can get sushi, rice, salad and soup for a set price. The early bird special, from 5 to7 p.m., is especially good and costs less than $8.00.

Whiz Burgers
700 So. Van Ness Ave. @ 18th St.

Whiz Burgers is the type of joint that when you randomly see it one day while riding your bicycle, you say to yourself, "Holy shit! How have I never seen this place before?" At least that's what happened to me. This spot is something out of a Beach Boys song or a movie starring a young Ron Howard. It's a walk up burger restaurant that's been around since 1955 and sells old-fashioned milkshakes. They have a variety of burger choices, including

ueen called Yamo Thai Kitchen, and one of those times it was an all-vegetarian place. Now it's just called Yamo, and it's a very tasty little hole-in-the-wall where nothing on the menu is over $5.25. It's a tiny place though, maybe eight seats max, so plan on waiting a little if it's a busy night.

Young's BBQ
3412 17th St. @ Valencia St.

If you want to have a hotdog and some chow-mein while reading National Geographic and hanging out with cops, then Young's BBQ is just the place for you. *What?* Yes, I meant exactly what I said. This oddly decorated hole in the wall sells Asian and American food, sits right across the street from the police station, and has more copies of National Geographic than all of the offices in the downtown medical-dental building put together.

Bars

500 Club
500 Guerrero St. @ 17th St.

A neon martini glass sign beckons you to this classic Mission dive bar where drinks are cheap and sometimes god-awful (the well whiskey tastes like tequila). The patrons here are a great mix of everything that the Mission and the Castro have to offer, and the bartenders can be friendly if the bar isn't crowded. I actually wasn't completely surprised when, at a newsstand in Montreal, I picked up a copy of *Stuff* magazine and saw that it had ranked the 500 Club as one of the top dive bars in the nation.

Amnesia
853 Valencia St. @ 19th St.
www.amnesiathebar.com

If my failing and soggy memory serves me correctly, I'm pretty sure Amnesia was the first bar I ever went to in San Francisco. I was 21 and had come up from Santa Cruz to interview for an internship at Bill Graham Presents. I remember loving the atmosphere and bugging out on the fact that the DJ was playing some of the hardest soul and rare grooves I'd ever heard. I'm pretty sure I danced like a complete fool that night and loved every minute of it. That's pretty much the story with Amnesia; the décor and vibe are pretty close to perfect, and every night of the week they have some type of great, often live, music going on (of course there is usually a small cover for the live music). I particularly like the gypsy jazz nights and the bluegrass nights. Wednesday nights are usually free and feature one of the Bay Area's best open mic/jazz sessions. They also have good Belgian beer on tap, but unfortunately there is no hard liquor.

Delirium

3139 16th St. @ Valencia St.

Delirium is one of the many dive bars in the vicinity of the 16"

...usually a DJ playing records. The bar also has stiff, cheap drinks. Oh yeah, I already mentioned that part.

El Rio

3158 Mission St. @ Valencia St.

It's hard to describe El Rio as anything short of awesome. The friendly crowd ranges from gay bikers to straight yuppies, and the bar sports a great patio to escape the madness of the inside. Whether it's salsa dancing or emaciated indie-rock, El Rio has something different going on every night of the week, including great deals. On Mondays, well drinks are $2 and Pabst is $1, but if you really want to start your weekend off right, get to El Rio between 5 and 7 p.m. on Friday and eat some free oysters.

The Elbo Room

647 Valencia St. @ 18th St.

www.elbo.com

This bar gets really good shows, but one of the cool things about it is that, although you do have to pay admission to go upstairs and see the band, you can just drink at the bar downstairs without paying a cover. The drinks are usually strong enough and the crowd is pretty chill. It's always a happening spot in the Mission. The bar has good drink deals like any other happy hour, but what makes this one special is that it goes from 5 p.m. all the way to 9 p.m., giving you four hours to start your night cheaply. Gotta love it.

Kilowatt
3160 16ᵗʰ St. @ Guerrero St.

Quite simply, Kilowatt is a good place to get drunk. This ex-venue consistently has some of the best-priced drinks in the city and the bartenders pour them heavy-handedly. The last time I was in there, a strong whiskey and 7-Up was only $3.50. There are plenty of other ways to amuse yourself at Kilowatt too. For instance, if you go in on your birthday, they'll give you a bottle of champagne and a Polaroid with one roll of film to use throughout the night. There is also a good jukebox, a few pool tables, pinball machines, and darts, and it never fails that any conversation can suddenly be interrupted by someone wanting to talk about Metallica. Yeah guy, you know who you are.

La Rondalla
901 Valencia St. @ 20ᵗʰ St.

This is the type of place where you take someone (a date or out of town guests) if you want to impress them with your hipness. "Why?" you ask. Because La Rondalla is one of the coolest places *ever!!* Every night, except for Mondays when they're closed, there is a live seven-piece Mariachi band, and they are fucking great! The decor has a yuletide feel because of all the tinsel and Christmas lights. By themselves the drinks are nothing special, but wait—I have a little secret for you: buy a pitcher of margaritas. They are only like $12 and are strong enough to get four aspiring alcoholics buzzed. A single pitcher by yourself might just kill you. The only real problem with La Rondalla is that seating is very limited unless you sit in the restaurant and buy food.

The Lexington Club
3464 19ᵗʰ St. @ Lexington St.

This divey Mission spot is probably the number one lesbian bar in San Francisco. It's got a decent jukebox and a pool table but not a lot of seating. The bartenders in this small place pour strong, moderately-priced drinks, and if it seems like everyone here knows each other, it's probably because they used to date. There's nothing glamorous about the Lexington Club, but if you're a woman who's looking to meet some ladies, there isn't a better spot in San Francisco.

⎯ ... ₌ ₌ some of the Mission's other watering holes, the place makes up for it in atmosphere, nice bartenders and munchies. The bar is low lit with little round tables sporting candles, and the sole TV in the place shows nothing but classic black and white movies on mute. The bartenders have superb taste in music, and best of all, they have all sorts of things to munch on, from Chex mix to peanuts. Do me a favor: If you meet a regular there named JT, buy him a drink; he's a good guy.

Phone Booth
1398 So. Van Ness Ave. @ 25th St.

This is one of those places where someone might want to beat me up for exposing their little drinking hole to the rest of the world. If that's the case, I'm just warning you that I pack heat. Just kidding, please don't beat me up. Anyway, the Phone Booth makes up for its diminutive size by having an overwhelming amount of character. The bartenders serve stiff, cheap drinks that you can chase with free popcorn while admiring the Tom Sellick picture and Barbie doll chandelier that you wish you'd made. What's also great about the Phone Booth is that although it is pretty hipsterish, the clientele is a perfect mix of gay, straight and everything in between.

Zeitgeist
199 Valencia St. @ Duboce St.

There are many reasons why Zeitgeist is one of the best bars in San Francisco. To begin with, the drinks are pretty cheap, pretty strong and can be super-sized to a pint glass (YES!). The place is also gargantuan. The inside is the size of a regular bar, but then there is a giant backyard complete with picnic tables and port-o-potties. I guess it is kinda a bike messenger bar (they have lots of bike racks), but all walks of life pass through the doors of Zeitgeist. And if you are too drunk to make it home, there is a hotel upstairs. I forgot to mention that they barbecue their own food too, making it a great place to spend a sunny Sunday after-noon. Also, don't take it personally if the bartenders are rude to you—they're like that to everyone.

Shopping

....

\ ....g spent most of that time in Argentina), I walked into this shop elated at the possibility of scoring some dulce de leche or some alfajores. Nah dude, they ain't got that shit here. What I found instead was a couple old guys taking turns talking shit into the telephone, in both Spanish and English, and racks full of soccer jerseys and flags. That's it. So if you need a new Italy jersey or a Guatemalan flag, you now know where to go.

Clothes Contact
473 Valencia St. @ 16th St.

This is one of the best places in the City to get some good looking, cheap clothes. As the sign says outside, Clothes Contact sells "Vintage by the Pound". This means that they weigh out the clothes that you wish to purchase and sell them according to that weight. If I'm not mistaken, the current going rate for a pound of clothes is around $10, which means you can probably get a great vintage shirt for super cheap.

Dog Eared Books
900 Valencia St. @ 20th St.

One of the many great bookstores that the Mission has to offer, Dog Eared carries mostly used books that range the whole gamut of possible literary subjects. The store has a nice, funky feel to it that seems to encourage long-term browsing, and their selection of comics and zines (including this book in a previous incarnation) is quite tasty. I really like the staff here too because, unlike some of the neighboring bookstores (which will remain nameless), they are very friendly, unpretentious and sweet people. Dog Eared is actually the first place I ever did a reading of any of my stuff. In 2006, they started a local writer reading series and asked me to

take part in the very first one. This astounded and flattered me because as far as I knew, I only wrote bathroom reading material. I read "Treading Through the Treacherous Tenderloin" which I ended up including in this here book that you're holding. Maybe if you invite me to your house I'll come read it for you too. You just have to supply cupcakes and wine like Dog Eared Books did.

If I wasn't illiterate, I would totally buy books here.

Martin's 16ᵗʰ St. Emporium
3248 16ᵗʰ St. @ Dolores St.

Martin is a semi-retired jeweler who has a fascination with skulls. He carries all kinds of weird shit, mostly stuff like candy skulls, silver skulls, inflatable skulls, etc. But he also carries a nice selection of decently priced eccentric jewelry. According to the business card they "have VERY unusual items. You will never see a store like this." I might have to agree. Even its hours are strange; it's only open Thursday through Saturday, 12 to 5 p.m.

Needles & Pens
3253 16ᵗʰ St. @ Guerrero St.

You've gotta love the Mission. I mean where else would you find a store like this? Needles & Pens is a remarkable shop that sells D.I.Y. goods like clothes and zines, and has a little art gallery as well. For those of you who don't know and who have never read *anything* about punk in the 70's, D.I.Y. stands for "Do It Yourself". Stop in at this tiny store to support local artists. Just remember

is completely free. My favorites are the full-sized female lion and the giraffe's head. What if I listed this as a vegan restaurant and suddenly all these vegans and veggies start showing up for what they're imagining to be a lovely lunch, only to be stared down by a row of bison and antelope heads? Would that be funny or fucked-up? Probably a little bit of both, huh?

Pedal Revolution
3085 21st St. @ So. Van Ness Ave.

San Francisco is a great town for bicycling in (if you don't mind some fucking serious hills). The folks at Pedal Revolution make this easier for you by taking shitty bikes and making them better, then selling them at fair prices. They also put together crazy little mutant bikes at the end of the summer for Burning Man.

Yoruba
998 Valencia St. @ 21st St.

This is basically a place to buy goods pertaining to Voodoo, Santeria and Yoruba. No joke. This isn't a little novelty store with preassembled Voodoo dolls and magic potions, this is a genuine practitioner's shop where you can buy all sorts of candles, oils, ingredients, etc. for your ritualistic needs. You can also get spiritual advice or readings. You gotta love the Mission. Where else would you find something this special?

↓

Sights & Entertainment

12 Galaxies
2565 Mission St. @ 22nd St.

Named after local legend and weirdo Frank Chu and his famous signs (see the Eye Spy Game), this Mission venue is a great place to see live music. Granted there is always a cover charge, but seriously—how many venues exist that don't have a cover? Whoever books the shows here has a very diverse musical palate because the shows range from ten-year-olds doing *School of Rock* type stuff, to weird thrash metal to hip-hop. You can see the stage from both floors, and the top one has both pool and video games. That way, if the band sucks but you got dragged by your buddy who's being creepy and kinda stalking the bartender, at least there is something to keep you occupied. www.12galaxies.com

Dolores Park
18th St. @ Dolores St.

One of the really cool things about this park is that it is basically where the Castro, the Mission, and Noe Valley meet. So on any given sunny day the park becomes a great cross-section of the entire city. If you go to the top of the park (it's on a hill) you get a big view of downtown and the bay, and if it is sunny you get a view of more men in Speedos than a European high school swim meet. Hey, whatever floats your boat.

The Golden Fire Hydrant
20th St. @ Church St.

During the 1906 earthquake and fire that destroyed much of San Francisco, this little fella was the only fire hydrant in the area

Ahh Dolores Park. Looking at this photo makes me wish I sold Speedos.

around the Mission that didn't completely crap-out. This fire hydrant single-handedly saved the entire area south of 20th St. from burning. In gratitude, it was painted gold and is ceremoniously repainted every April 18th on the anniversary of the earthquake.

Hua Zang Si Buddhist Temple

3134 22nd St. @ So. Van Ness Ave.

I like to wander. It's really one of my favorite things to do. You know, just kinda going for a walk and seeing what kind of cool shit I come across. Well for awhile I always noticed this humongous red church on 22nd St. and it reminded me of some of the architecture I saw in Munich, so I just figured it's some sort of German church. Then, just the other day, I took a closer look and had to ask myself, "Shit, when did the Germans start writing in Chinese and having big-ass statues of Buddha in the foyers of their churches?" When I saw the sign that said "free admission", I knew I didn't have a choice (curiosity is a sign of intelligence, right?). So I went inside and was delighted; there was a superb art exhibit by some very holy man, and a few of the biggest Buddha statues I'd ever seen in person. One of them had to be close to two stories tall. Apparently the place was a German Lutheran church built around 1900 and the Buddhists kept the original organ pipes and stained glass windows when they took it over. Man, the nuns in there loved me! They were very sweet and happily answered all of my questions. They were just so excited that I came and checked out their spot. So was I.

Precita Eyes
2981 24th St.@ Harrison St.

One of the things that the Mission is famous for is the abundance of murals on the walls of business and public buildings through-out the neighborhood. Precita Eyes has been responsible for a great deal of these beautiful murals ever since its beginnings as an art collective in the mid 70's. If you have any interest in murals at all, stop in at the Precita Eyes Mural Arts Center where you can pick up supplies, take classes and even join a walking tour of many of the Mission's murals.

Theatre Rhinoceros
2926 16th St. @ Mission St.
www.therhino.org

Having been around since 1977, Theatre Rhinoceros is the world's longest running Queer theater troupe. Their plays examine the many multi-faceted issues of being Queer in American society. Since they feel that theater is something that all people should have access to, they have "pay as you can" preview performances at the beginning of a show's run. For more info about Theatre Rhinoceros, call (415) 861-5079.

San Francisco Facts

All of these facts either ~~~~ f~ ~~~ ~~~

- The population is 739,426.

- San Francisco is the only place in the country where the city and the county it's in have the same borders.

- The City is 7 miles by 7 miles (which is where the awful local magazine 7x7 got its name).

- SF has 14 sister cities, including Haifa, Israel; Ho Chi Minh, Vietnam and Cork, Ireland.

- The City's motto is "Oro en Paz, Fierro en Guerra" which means "Gold in Peace, Iron in War" in some language that's not English.

- 35% of the population is Catholic, 22% is Jewish, 18% is pagan, while another 7% of San Francisco's population considers their religion to be Jedi.

- San Francisco has 20 billionaires. I'm not one of them. Chances are, neither are you.

- The Mayor is Gavin Newsom, who is famous for sanctioning gay marriage and for having the self-control of Cookie Monster.

MISSION
Detail Area

16TH ST

18TH

19TH

20TH

LIBERTY ST

GUERRERO

VALENCIA

LEXINGTON

SAN

MISSION

CARLOS

21ST ST

ID

Mission
Playground
and Pool

4:00 AM

N

0   0.2 miles
0   0.3 kilometers

©2007 Angela Hathaway, SF

THE MISSION

GRUB-A-DUB-DUB

1 Atlas Cafe
2 Big Mouth Burgers
3 China Express
4 El Cachanilla
5 El Trebol Restaurant
6 Pancho Villa's
7 Que Tal
8 Red Cafe
9 Revolution Cafe
10 Ritual
11 Serrano's Pizza
12 Smile BBQ
13 St. Francis Fountain
14 The Tamale Lady
15 Tartine
16 Tortas El Primo
17 Tortilla Flats
18 We Be Sushi
19 Whiz Burgers
20 Yamo
21 Young's B.B.Q
22 Cha Cha Cha
23 OSHA Thai Noodle House

FREE FOOD!

24 Last Supper Club
25 El Rio

VEGGIE FRIENDLY FOOD

26 Cafe Gratitude
27 Cha-Ya
28 Herbivore
29 Little Otsu
30 Minako Organic Japanese Restaurant
31 Rainbow Grocery

LATE NITE EATS

32 El Farolito
33 New Yorker's Buffalo Wings

THE MISSION

 PLACES TO CHECK OUT

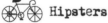 SHOPPING

 Hipsters

Helado (ice cream) cart dude

 Fake ID Guy

The Tenderloin/ TenderNob

Although it's exact boundaries are forever a point of contention for those living there, the Tenderloin, for all intents and purposes, is the space running east/west between Van Ness Avenue and Mason Street, and north/south between Geary Boulevard and Market Street. Rumor has it that the Loin, as it is affectionately called, got its name back in the day when dirty cops would accept bribes to look the other way to the shady dealings of the neighborhood. Just as a tenderloin is one of the best cuts of meat, the Tenderloin was one of the best cuts of the city. At least that's what some old cab driver told me. Anyway, the Loin is now more or less San Francisco's skid row. It is full of crack-heads, junkies, residential hotels, homeless people and poor immigrant families who are trying to get the hell out. But with all this said, it is also home to some of the best cheap restaurants and bars in all of San Francisco. To be honest, it's one of the places I used to spend most of my time in. But still, I don't recommend going too deep into the Loin by yourself at night, *especially* if you are a woman. The area is not exactly super-dangerous; it's just that you have to be more aware of your surroundings.

As you may ascertain from the name, the TenderNob is the space between the lovely Loin and Nob Hill. This area is not as shady as the Loin, not as nice as Nob Hill, and is probably one of the best locations in San Francisco simply because of its proximity to everything.

Also squeezed into this section are the things residing in Polk Gulch (kinda like Tenderloin light) and Hayes Valley (a bastion of upscale shopping and eating, surrounded by housing projects).

Food

...and it's open 24 hours. (It's always good to know as many different 24 hour spots as possible.) Another thing about Café Mason is that it's located right next to an international youth hostel, so there are always interesting people hanging around, and they seem to hire almost exclusively cute foreign girls. I don't know what else to say about this place so...I guess that's it.

Cordon Bleu Restaurant
1574 California St. @ Polk St.

I popped into this tiny hole-in-the-wall for lunch the other day and walked away very pleased, very full and slightly less hungover than when I had entered. For five bucks I got a giant piece of five-spice chicken, country salad (a fancy-pants name for coleslaw), and meat sauce over rice. The menu claims that the five-spice chicken is "Possibly the best chicken you will ever have outside of Vietnam" and while I may not necessarily agree (I've never been to Vietnam), it is damn good. For me though, the real kicker was the meat sauce. The only way I could properly describe it is—fortifying. I think that shit could cure cancer.

El Super Burrito
1200 Polk St. @ Sutter St.

While some Mexican food restaurants have fancy and romantic names like El Farolito or Taqueria Cancun, the people at El Super Burrito said, "Fuck that! Let's have our name tell people exactly what we do; we make big motherfucking burritos. That's what we do!" It'd be like a clothing store being named Very Comfortable Cotton T-shirts (believe it or not, one of the world's biggest telescopes is actually called the Very Large Telescope. These people can design a way to see light years away, yet can't think of anything better than Very Large Telescope). Despite the uncreative name, the burritos here are good and yes, very big. The jumbo burrito is easily big enough for two people to split and it's only $5.50. They also have all-you-can-eat chips and salsa. But the decoration here takes the cake—they have so many Corona streamers and piñatas hung up that you would think it was a five-year-old kid named Corona's birthday party.

Food & Liquor World

728 Post St. between Leavenworth & Jones Sts.

In San Francisco there are plenty of corner stores where you can pop in to pick up your basic needs like beer, Cheetos, porno mags, etc., and from the outside, Food & Liquor World seems like just another of these shops. But once you step inside, it's quite different. Besides the aforementioned amenities, you can find pretty much anything a household could need, from kitty litter to chicken noodle soup. They also have a full grill and deli that offers excellent, well-priced food specials every day. The grilled chicken sandwich is scrumptious and the freshly made hummus is fucking delectable. The very near vicinity houses many international students, making Food & Liquor World a great place to meet sexy foreign nationals. And if all this isn't enough to get you in there, the guys who run it are some of the nicest folks in San Francisco—honestly.

Golden Coffee

901 Sutter St. @ Leavenworth St.

Located at the corner of Sutter and Leavenworth, Golden Coffee is probably one of the best-priced diners in all of San Francisco. If you are broke as hell but don't feel like cooking, this is the place for you. You can get two eggs, four strips of bacon, hash browns and toast for like $4.50. But Golden Coffee's hours are only from 7 a.m. to 4 p.m., so you might have to find dinner someplace else.

......ays an interesting one. Also, ...c.....or has this weird Portuguese nautical thing going on. But everything said and done, this is a great place with really good food and fair prices. They also happen to have what I feel are the best damn mozzarella sticks this side of the Mississippi.

Hahn's Coffee Shop
900 Sutter St. @ Leavenworth St.

This guy sits directly across the street from Golden Coffee; I almost feel like it's a duel or something. The prices are very similar to Golden Coffee, but I haven't actually eaten there, so I can't vouch for how good it is. Go eat there and drop me a line telling me how it was.

Little Henry's
955 Larkin St. @ Post St.

If you want a good, hearty Italian dining experience, then North Beach is one of the best places you can go on the west coast. But if you want cheap Italian food, cooked and served by an all-Cambodian staff, then Little Henry's in the Tenderloin is your spot. Go there for lunch and get chicken Parmesan, salad, pasta, bread and a drink for around $6.25. As with most things, you get what you pay for, but at least in this case, you get pretty full.

Nara Sushi
1515 Polk St. @ California St.

A lot of people talk about how good Nara is and I'd have to agree with them. The sushi here is very fresh and they occasionally do cool stuff like play movies on the wall. What also makes them great is that they have $20 all-you-can-eat sushi most nights of the week. I can eat a grip of sushi, so this makes me happy.

New Village Café
1426 Polk St. @ California St.

This is a good place to sit at the counter and unload your worries by scribbling random things on the paper napkins while eating cheap food. What—you don't do that? The walls of this place are lined with photos of the joint's regular customers, but really the best things to look at are the crazy speed freaks who lurk outside and holler weird shit at people stopping in to scribble their worries onto paper napkins while eating cheap food.

Original Joe's
144 Taylor St. @ Eddy St.

The decor of this spacious Italian/American restaurant harkens back to a time when the Tenderloin was a little bit more tender and smelled a lot less of piss. At Original Joe's, not much has changed since 1937: the waiters still wear tuxes, the booths are large, the cocktail lounge is swanky, and you can sit at the lunch counter if you like. Eating here feels like being in a Frank Sinatra song. Although this is definitely not the cheapest place in the Loin (it's about $12 for an entree), the portions are big enough to share with the guy who plans on mugging you on your way out. Really though, if you want a good meal and can spare a few extra bucks, go to Original Joe's.

P.S. Word to my dad who turned me on to this place; it's his favorite restaurant in the City.

This guy's not just winking because the food is good. He's winking because he sees something you don't, namely the crackhead who's about to brain you with a brick and take your wallet.

Piccadilly Fish & Chips

1348 Polk St. @ Pine St.

In the UK and Ireland (and probably Australia and New Zealand too) they call these places chippers. Here in the States we call them, "you know, fish and chips places, man". Regardless of what you call them, fish and chips is some damn good shit to put in your belly after you've been doing some drinking. My only real complaint about this chipper (other than the fact that it closes at midnight on the weekends) is that it kinda makes the entire block reek like greasy, fried funk.

Osha Thai Noodle

696 Geary Blvd. @ Leavenworth St.; *also*
819 Valencia St. @19th St, 2033 Union St. @
Buchanan St., 149 2nd St. @ Minna St.

Open really late, this noodle house has very fast service and very good food. I usually get the Pineapple Fried Rice, which comes with shrimp and chicken, for like $7. This place is always happening on Friday and Saturday nights. It's worth putting up with the shitty music because it's that great a place. The menus at each location are neighborhood-specific, meaning that the one in the Loin is the cheapest one. Know what I mean?

Pinecrest Diner

401 Geary Blvd. @ Mason St.

This is a simple, classic diner open 24 hours. The crowd here is always interesting to say the least. Some of them drank their way over from Union Square, some realized it was their last chance for food on the way home, and some people have scrounged up enough money to buy a cup of coffee so that they have a place to sit inside for a couple hours. Anyway, the food isn't exactly cheap and it's pretty fucking not good, but it is open 24/7. I usually opt for the chili, which rings in at about $5. An interesting bit of info is that in 1997, one of the cooks shot a waitress to death because she berated him about making poached eggs since they weren't on the menu.

P.S. Thanks to Mr. SF for that last tid-bit of info.
(*www.mrsf.com*)

Saigon Sandwiches

560 Larkin St. @ Eddy St.

Like many little Vietnamese sandwich places in the Loin, Saigon Sandwiches is ridiculously cheap. Most sandwiches are $2.25 and a few of them are $3. There you go.

Sliders Diner

1205 Sutter St. @ Polk St.

(See entry on page 245)

Sunny Café

1338 Polk St. @ Pine St.

Just your typical Polk Street greasy spoon diner. The most expensive thing on the menu is the $7.50 Cobb Salad. Burgers are $4.15. If you figure out anything else notable about it, I'd love to know.

Tommy's Joynt
1101 C~~ ~

..... ιι also has an ungodly selection of beers from all over the world that are almost as well priced as they are tasty. Tommy's earns more cool points because their hearty food is served cafeteria style and is tremendously affordable. All this, combined with the weird shit on the walls inside and the colorful painting on the walls outside, is what has made Tommy's Joynt one of the best spots in San Francisco since 1947.

I now know why everyone hates going to dinner with me; I play with my food, write my name in mustard and start poking people with french fries. Jesus, I'm a fucking asshole. Photo by Victoria Smith

Turk & Larkin Deli
467 Turk St. @ Larkin St.

Walking into this wood-paneled lunch spot, you get the feeling that the only thing that has changed since its 1979 opening is the rest of the world. It looks like the type of place where Travis Bickel (De Niro's character from *Taxi Driver*) would hang out between fares, if that makes any sense. The food here is pretty good and affordable (sandwiches are less than $5) and the clientele is not as smelly as one would expect. If you're in the neighborhood, stop in for a bite, but note that they are only open Monday through Friday till 3:30 p.m. If you owned a business in this neighborhood would you want to be open any later?

Wrap Delight
426 Larkin St. @ Turk St.

This place is amazing solely because their menu, consisting of over 40 sandwiches, has nothing on it over $2.75. This tiny little walk-in deli, like any Vietnamese sandwich shop, has the obligatory barbecued pork and chicken sandwiches, but it also has a wide variety of other more commonplace sandwiches. It's located close enough to city hall that you can go before or after any of the many protests that happen in SF.

Bars

......g ren-

.....gmy 10:30 p.m.; needless to say I was pretty drunk. Despite this, I was not prepared to look out the window and see a middle-aged Asian guy with orange, battery powered, glowing/blinking glasses, who was waving a wand crowned with an equally luminescent snow-globe type thing. He was also pushing around three huge duffel bags on a cart, each filled with more glowing/blinking toys. I'm pretty sure the guy had accidentally stepped through a wormhole and was actually from another dimension. Just when I said "Who the hell in the *Tenderloin* is gonna buy that shit?", my friend Kenny walked in with his own pair of glasses and a wand. The Loin is a strange fucking place at night, and Club 21 is a great spot to meet some of its most interesting characters.

Aunt Charlie's Lounge
133 Turk St. @ Taylor St.

Aunt Charlie's is where old drag queens go to die. Even if you've seen hundreds of drag shows, this one will stick with you for the rest of your life. Anything else I might say would just cheapen your Aunt Charlie's experience.

The Brown Jug
496 Eddy St. @ Hyde St.

(see the story on page 75)

Club 65

65 Taylor St. @ Golden Gate Ave.

The sole reason I went to Club 65 last night was to find out whether or not a certain man existed. Apparently more of a fixture at the bar than a patron, "The General", as he's called, is rumored to be an ancient one-eyed creature, with great big long fingernails, a mane of white hair, and the biggest belt buckle a human has ever worn. Unfortunately, I didn't catch him, but I did manage to drink some very strong, cheap drinks. I feel like "The General" is quickly becoming my Moby Dick and that if I don't come across him soon, my life will be worthless. Looks like I'll have to get some drinks in the Loin again tonight. Wanna come too?

Edinburgh Castle

950 Geary Blvd. between Polk St. & So. Van Ness Ave.

www.castlenews.com

Edinburgh Castle is one of the most unique bars that San Francisco has to offer. It is goddamn huge, has pool and darts, a separate area for shows, cheap strong drinks, smelly bathrooms, stellar fish and chips, and a buzzing literary scene that includes *Trainspotting* author Irvine Welsh. The patrons of this bar are a good mix of young, hip kids and Scottish ex-pats, and the motif is that of a castle. Pretty cool, huh?

Hemlock Tavern

1131 Polk St. between Sutter & Post Sts.

www.hemlocktavern.com

A scenester's dream, the Hemlock Tavern is full of people who are "in a band". But regardless of the sometimes full-of-shit clientele, the Tavern has well poured decently-priced drinks and live music every night. Generally there is no show over $10 and you can still go in the bar for free and not see the show. There is also a semi-enclosed smoking area, so you can drink and smoke at the same time. But the best part of the Tavern is that for a buck you can buy a bag of warm peanuts. If you've never had warm nuts, you're missing out on some serious stuff.

Hightide

600 G---- --- -

---..ght, is populated by upwardly mobile people who make a lot of money. This being said, it is one of the more aesthetically pleasing bars around and has an excellent happy hour. Inside the bar is this huge waterfall that goes from the second of the bar's three levels to the bottom one. The upper level is a lounge, the middle one has a bar and the lower one has a bar and a lounge. And the coolest thing of all is that in the men's room there is a one-way mirror that looks out into the bar. To top it off, at happy hour, well drinks, some specialty drinks and most beers are only $2. It is definitely worth checking this place out.

Jonell's

401 Ellis St. @ Jones St.

(see the story on page 72)

O'Farrell Street Bar

800 Larkin St. @ O'Farrell St.

Despite the puke by the urinal and the holes punched into the bathroom wall, this place looks a lot better than the last time I was here. Maybe it's the new paint job. Either way, they still have $3 Budweisers, a couple pool tables and that cool fish tank where the fish are always kissing each other and occasionally swimming sideways.

Vertigo
1160 Polk St. @ Sutter St.

The tropically-themed Vertigo is a nice retreat from the transvestite hookers and urine-smelling streets that surround the area. Vertigo's decor is awesome, with an apparently hand carved wooden bar, lazy Tahitian-like fans, and a great covered tropical smoking patio. One of the unique things about this place is that they specialize in drinks for multiple people. The Volcano costs something like $18.50 but is a monstrous thing made for four (or two if you're alcoholics). And they have drink specials on many nights. On Tuesdays there are DJs with no cover charge, and they have $1 beers and $4 martinis. Also, early in the week Pabst is only $1.

Whiskey Thieves
839 Geary Blvd. @ Larkin St.

(see the story on page 72)

The White Horse Pub
635 Sutter St. @ Taylor St.

There are many happy hours in the City that provide good, cheap drinks. But there are few that provide good cheap food. The White Horse Pub provides good FREE food every Monday. Starting at 5:30, they serve FREE chicken wings and chili and fried wontons and all you have to do is buy a drink. Although the drinks are regularly priced, you can buy a single beer and eat for free.

Shopping

, ..., house wares, socks, telephones, *tear gas,* walkman and CD"? The italics are mine, but really, *TEAR GAS?* That is awesome! To my dismay though, the tear gas was actually in a mace/pepper spray form and not the tear gas grenades I was looking for. But the upside is I found a switchblade instead. You've gotta love the Tenderloin.

Bibliohead Bookstore
334 Gough St. @ Hayes St.

In an age when independent bookstores are falling by the wayside like polio victims in a marathon, it's always heartening to see a bookstore that is doing alright for itself. Bibliohead stands among the glitz of Hayes Valley, selling its new, used and rare wares while pounding its chest and singing "We Shall Overcome". Okay, that's a little melodramatic, but this is a great bookstore that you should definitely shop at. I know you're getting sick of me saying this, but please support independent businesses, especially bookstores, because otherwise your only option will be to buy whatever Borders sees fit to sell you.

Brand Fury
780 Sutter St. @ Jones St.

A toy store for adults (get your mind out of the gutter), Brand Fury sells things like Bruce Lee action figures and toys based on Japanimation cartoons. It's kinda like a comic book store without all the comic books. Although the toys are pricey, the people at Brand Fury for some reason have all kinds of cool swag—like movie tickets and records—to give away.

European Book Company
925 Larkin St. @ Geary Blvd.

Okay, so technically it can be said that they sell books in French, German and Spanish but really it's more of a French language bookstore that dabbles in other tongues. Somebody told me that San Francisco has a pretty sizable population of French ex-pats, which might explain the existence of this store, but considering its location, they'd probably make a lot more money selling crack rocks than *Tin-Tin* books.

International College of Cosmetology II
1224 Polk St. @ Bush St.

The positive thing about this place is that everything is super cheap. Men's haircuts are $5 while women's are $7 and up. You can also get a pedicure for only $10 and even—if you so dare—get your bikini line waxed for $20. The downside of this place is that everyone here is in training, meaning that there is a definite chance they might completely fuck up and you'd be walking around San Francisco with a retarded looking haircut, a half waxed bikini line and poorly painted toenails. As of yet I haven't tried the place, but I certainly could use a pedicure.

Isotope Comics
326 Fell St. @ Gough St.

Isotope might be the only "Comic Book Lounge" in the world and it's definitely the only one in the City. Seriously, who thought a comic book store could be so cool? Unlike most other comic book stores, which are generally cluttered and small, Isotope is a big open space, with comfy leather lounge chairs, neat interior design and a great selection of graphic novels, comics and zines from all over the Bay Area and around the world. Another unique thing about Isotope is that the staff is doing wonders in regards to the image of a comic book store clerk. These folks are really unpretentious, cool and accessible people. And of course the best thing about Isotope is the man behind the m̲a̲d̲n̲e̲s̲s̲.

̲.̲.̲.̲ young and specific bookstores in the City, Kayo specializes in paperback pulp fiction and dime novels from the 1940s up through the 70s. The selection that they have is astounding and the prices are pretty reasonable. I especially like all the obscure and vintage porn that this store sells, but then again, I'm a pervert. Kayo is also one of John Waters' favorite stores in San Francisco. If you don't believe me, go check it out. They'd love to tell you about it. Just remember that they're only open Thursday through Saturday.

The Magazine
920 Larkin St. @ Cedar St.

Wow—I'm really amazed people don't talk about this one more. It's definitely one of those places that deserves mention in as many conversations as possible. It literally has one of the biggest archives of porno mags I've ever seen, and what's remarkable is the sheer variety. If you're into 18-year-old Inuit virgins in clown suits being drenched in hot coffee, there's a 97% chance that The Magazine has what you're looking for. Sure this store has old fishing and baking magazines and shit for like $0.35, but who cares about that when there are back issues of *Juggs*? If you don't dig this place, you seriously have no soul (or a strong aversion to dirty old pervs).

Quick Printing
1288 Polk St. @ Bush St.

Let's say that you wanted to write a zine. And let's just say that it was about all the great cheap, fun things to do in San Francisco and that you called it *Broke-Ass Stuart's Guide to Living Cheaply in San Francisco* (which you can't because I copyrighted it, bitches!). Then I would recommend you getting your zine published by the fine people of Quick Printing. My main man, John, took care of my zine printing needs once I realized that I'd been buttfucked (that is a technical financial term if I'm not mistaken) by Kinko's. Although there are a few Quick Printers in the City, each one is individually owned. So if you need to get some printing done, go see the folks at the Polk Street location—they're good people. Not that it will change anything, but tell them Broke-Ass Stuart sent you; you'll at least get a chuckle.

RAG
541 Octavia St. @ Grove St.

RAG, which stands for Residents Apparel Gallery, is not what I would conventionally call cheap, but considering that it is the best priced place in the City to purchase clothes designed by Bay Area independent designers, it's really well priced in the relative sense. The clothes here are amazing, the staff is super friendly, helpful and cute, and where else are you gonna get such unique stuff at these prices?

↓

Sights & Entertainment

the largest art-by-Asian-people collections in the world. It's also in an impressive building that used to house San Francisco's main library. Admission is $12 but it's free on the first Tuesday of every month. I love you for buying this book. I promise you're not a sucker.

Cable Car Museum
1201 Mason St. @ Washington St.

Look, I know this one is actually in Nob Hill, but fuck it, it's close enough. If you haven't figured it out by the name, this is where you can come learn all about SF's most famous transit system (yeah that's right BART, you ain't shit) and its history. The building also houses the mechanisms that make the cable car system work. It's a small museum, but it's pretty cool and it's free. The one drawback is that it's almost impossible to get here without walking up some kind of hill.

City Hall
The big ass domed building at Civic Center

Here in the City, the area called Civic Center is really just a prettier name for the Tenderloin. I love meeting tourists who are staying around the Civic Center because they always say something like, "Yeah, the area is a little sketchy," which actually means, "I saw some of the craziest shit I've ever seen in my life last night. I can't believe that woman tried to sell me her baby." But the one thing that Civic Center has over the rest of the Loin is beautiful architecture, especially City Hall. This exquisite looking building was first built in 1915 and was fully renovated in 1999. If you go to City Hall, you can sign up for a walking tour, or feel free to walk around by yourself.

Crackheads
All over the Loin

If you've never seen someone smoking crack, here's you're chance, you sick fucking voyeur. The Tenderloin has got more crack than the Liberty Bell.

Glide Memorial United Methodist Church
330 Ellis St. @ Taylor St.

I'm an agnostic Jew, with no great love for organized religion, who considers himself Jewish because of 5,000 years of inherited culture (and motherly guilt). You follow? OK, with that being said, I think Glide might be one of the few examples of organized religion actually living up to its end of the deal and doing something beautiful and good for the world. Ever since Rev. Cecil Williams took the helm in 1963, Glide has been a haven for all people. On any given Sunday at Glide, you can be standing in the congregation and have a transsexual prostitute standing to your left, a millionaire to your right, a heroin addict in front of you, and a working single mother behind you. Rev. Williams' message is that God loves you exactly as you are. Personally, if I were to believe in God, that's the kind of God I would want to believe in. They also do an amazing amount of work for the surrounding Tenderloin community including daily free meals, health services, counseling, family services, and job training and employment. But all that aside, the real reason to visit Glide is to hear its choir. They could be singing the words of Ronald Reagan's inaugural address and it would still sound gorgeous.

The Great American Music Hall

859 O'Farrell St. @ Polk St.

www.musichallsf.com

In existe...

THE LOIN

9 Cordon Bleu
   Restaurant
10 Saigon Sandwiches
11 Turk & Larkin Deli
12 Wrap Delight
13 Sunny Cafe
14 New Village Cafe
15 El Super Burrito
16 Sliders Diner
17 Tommy's Joynt

 FREE FOOD!

18 Sugar Lounge

 VEGGIE FRIENDLY FOOD

19 Ananda Fuara
20 Mekong Restaurant

 LATE NITE EATS

21 Bob's Donut and
   Pastry Shop
22 Grubstake
23 Mel's Drive-In
24 Naan 'n Curry
25 OSHA Thai Noodle
26 Pinecrest Diner

 DRINKS DRINKS DRINKS

27 21 Club
28 The Brown Jug
29 Club 65
30 Edinburgh Castle
31 Hemlock Tavern
32 Hightide
33 Jonell's
34 O'Farrell Street
   Bar

40 City Hall
41 Great American
   Music Hall
42 Glide
43 Asian Art Museum

 SHOPPING

44 Alex's Gift Shop
45 Brand Fury
46 European Book
   Company
47 Kayo Books
48 Quick Printing
49 International
   College of
   Cosmetology II
50 The Magazine
51 Bibliohead
   Bookstore
52 Isotope Comics
53 RAG

💋 Ladies of the night

💋 "Ladies" of the night

💩 Dog poop

💩 People poop

💀 Crackheads

Treading Through the Treacherous Tenderloin

By Broke-Ass Stuart

The night was winding down at the mediocre Italian restaurant in North Beach. My last table had just walked out the door and Kenny was putting his final silverware roll-up in the appropriate basket. "How much longer do you have?" he asked.

I took a look at the list of closing duties, "All I've got left is to take out the trash and do my roll-ups. Are you still down to come out and do research with me?"

Kenny got up from the counter and laughed, "I love how you call it research. I am absolutely down."

This was the night that I had planned on researching the Tenderloin for volume two of *Broke-Ass Stuart's Guide to Living Cheaply in San Francisco*, and in this case "research" meant going to a bunch of different bars, taking notes and drinking. It's really a tough manner of work, one that in fact required me to make use of a research assistant. Luckily Kenny had an extensive background in this field and volunteered himself for this particular assignment (that is to say, we drank together a lot, and I needed some company). This wasn't going to be a regular night at the Hemlock Tavern talking to average-looking hipster chicks about bands I couldn't give a fuck about, no sir. This night we were hitting up some of the Loin's real dive bars, the types of places where the shit gets real thick on the first and fifteenth of every month. We left the restaurant around 10:30 p.m., walked a couple blocks down Columbus, turned right onto Stockton and followed the street all the way until we were spit out on the other end of its filthy tunnel. We turned onto Geary and it wasn't long before we were treading through the treacherous Tenderloin. It was at Geary and Jones that the neon lights of the Hightide

⸻ spoke mostly Maya and hailed from the Yucatan Peninsula. From time to time, groups of nubile young travelers would wander in from a nearby hostel, but the overall feeling of the place would never have been described as sexy. Walking into the Hightide that night, a step or two before Kenny, I was shocked by a drastic change that had occurred sometime in the year of my absence. I acknowledged this mildly: "Holy shit Kenny—there are girls in here and they're pretty!" Always an astute observer, Kenny had already picked up on this fact, replying, "From the looks of it, they have all of their teeth too. And I don't even see a single eye patch in the crowd."

"Aw, come on dude, I didn't make it out to be that bad, did I?" In fact, knowing my tendency to exaggerate, I probably had, but at that moment it was inconsequential. What mattered was that Kenny was right; there wasn't a single eye patch or missing tooth in the whole place. I'd have to make a note of that. "Anyways, what are you drinking? I'll get first round," I changed the subject as we were now sitting at the bar and clearly within earshot of most of its patrons.

A pretty bartender approached us and asked what we'd like. "I'll take a Madras please," I answered, and pointing to Kenny, said, "and also, whatever the good doctor would like."

He ordered his drink, "I'll take a Pabst please," and turned to me and asked, "What's a Madras?"

"It's vodka, cran, and orange juice," I answered, "I'm trying to be a little bit more healthy."

"Wait, wait, wait ... because orange juice and cranberry juice are both good for you, you're saying that the two combined must cancel out the awful things that the vodka does to your body?" he asked incredulously, and I nodded in agreement. "Wow! That has to be single handedly the most ridiculous and," he paused dramatically, "brilliant thing you've ever said." The drinks arrived and I paid the lady the measly price of six bucks plus tip.

"Denial is a beautiful thing, isn't it?" I took a sip and grimaced. The drinks were still stiff and cheap. I knew it was going to be a good night.

We left the Hightide and continued down Geary. I'd remembered that a new bar had opened up where Julep used to be, and I wanted to check it out. We found Whiskey Thieves almost completely empty; there were maybe ten people inside including the barkeep. Kenny got us each a Madras and we sat down at the back of the bar in order to soak up the atmosphere and take some notes. Enjoying my refreshing beverage I came to the conclusion that in a neighborhood full of dive bars, Whiskey Thieves kinda seemed like the new kid who was desperately trying to fit in. It was the type of place you'd go if you knew that you weren't prepared for the caliber of shit that the Tenderloin had to offer. But us, we were prepared, and we knew it, so we finished our drinks and decided that the next bar would be the type of place where people go to drink their lives away. We like comedy.

It took about three seconds after walking in the door at Jonell's to realize that this was exactly the spot we were looking for. Named so because it sits on the corner of Jones and Ellis, Jonell's is the type of fine establishment where sitting with your back to the door might be the last bad decision you ever make. The patrons are generally drunk and leery old men who piss away all their money on booze and hookers, but the vibe is actually far from inhospitable. In fact, if you sit down at the bar, expect to get an earful of some the most fucked up stories you've ever heard.

Settling down at the horseshoe-shaped bar, I saw a huge Samoan guy with a friendly but worn-looking face come out of the

bathroom carrying a bunch of cleaning supplies. "Jesus Christ,"
I said to Kenny, under my breath, "could you imagine having to
clean that bathroom? It's gotta be worse than a dumpster behind a
needle exchange."

man pushed through the door with the force of a house ripped
from the ground and blown to Oz. The bar was pretty empty, but I
knew he'd land right next to me. They always do.

Sitting down one stool away, the man said a round of hellos.
"Hey Suzy, hey Ricky," he greeted the couple who ran the bar.
Then he greeted the only other people in the bar besides me and
Kenny, a fat white guy who appeared to be completely catatonic,
and an old black guy in a straw fedora, "Hey Fred, hey Willis."
Finally he turned to us: "Hey new guys, I'm Mike." Before we got
a chance to introduce ourselves though, he began addressing the
whole bar.

"Oh man, I just came from this huge fucking party where
there was all this free food and free booze, and Jesus, shit man,
you shoulda seen all the pussy in this place. Ya see, this guy I
know, I gots all kinds of friends, this guy I know just opened
this Cuban restaurant and tonight was the opening party. It was
beautiful, my buddy really went all out, and the food, oh the food!
Better than anything I ever eaten, other than my mother's cooking
of course, God rest her sweet soul. This food was so good; I almost
went to the store to buy some sandwich bags so I could sneak
some out but I figured I didn't wanna look sleazy in front of all
those rich people. But fuck 'em anyways. Ya guys ever had Cuban
food? Them fucking Cubans really know how to shake some pots
and pans, ya know what I mean? Look, I even brought a menu so
you could see what I'm talkin bout. Here, pass it around." At this

point Mike pulled out a folded up paper menu and handed it to Suzy, the bartender who had just dropped off two Buds for Kenny and me, and a glass of whiskey for Mike. "Thanks Suzy, how'd ya know what I wanted?"

"Cuz you get the same damn drink every night," Suzy answered sweetly while taking the menu that Mike had handed her. Suzy read over the menu and then passed it around while Mike proudly looked on as if he were letting his friends touch a piece of the true cross he'd found in Jerusalem. The menu got around to me and, I'll have to admit, the food did sound pretty good.

"Looks good man," I answered his awaiting eyes. Mike looked like his 50 or 60 years on this Earth had been rough; you could tell he'd definitely been around the block a few times. But he was jolly in his roughness, and he was energetic and also pretty tubby. He kinda reminded me of an all grown up, alcoholic, bearded version of "Chunk" from *The Goonies*. I got the feeling that Mike was a good guy, just a little overzealous.

"You're fuckin-A right it looks good. And it tasted even better," he answered. "Ha! And shit man, the women in there were so hot they wouldn't a even fucked me when I was you're age. How old are ya, 21, 22? What are young bloods like you doing in here anyways? If you're looking for pussy, this ain't the place, but you can buy some pussy on Polk Street if you want. Be careful though; check for an Adam's apple, cuz some of them women ain't exactly women. Know what I mean?" He followed this with a wink. "But then again maybe you're into that fag shit anyways. If you is, it don't bother me none, but from the looks of it," he gestured around the room, "you ain't gonna get any dick in here either. Except for maybe Fred, I don't know cuz that son-of-a-bitch don't talk. Now what'd ya say you guys are doing here?"

I took the last sip of my beer and made the international sign for "two more" to Suzy. Then I turned to Mike, "Well we're here doing some research. I do this book/zine/guide thingy called 'Broke-Ass Stuart's Guide to Living Cheaply in San Francisco', and we're out here doing research for volume two. Jonell's seemed like a perfect place for my book." At this point I pulled out a copy and showed it to him.

"So by research you mean you're going around to a bunch of different bars, drinking, and taking notes," Mike asked. He was

ﬂ̲̲̲̲̲̲̲̲̲̲̲̲̲̲̲̲̲̲

Five bucks," I said. I couldn't believe I was making a sale in Jonell's of all places.

"Well, I've got your Fin right here, and I'll do you one even better." He put the five dollar note on the table in front of me and proceeded: "The best bar in the world is just a few blocks from here. You ever heard of the Brown Jug over on Eddy and Hyde? Best bar in the world. My old lady's been working there for 22 years. Beautiful American-Indian broad. We been married 30 years, can you believe that? Man they got some nice atmosphere in there and a great jukebox, and boy, my old lady can really pour a drink. Take my advice," he looked down at the book, "Broke-Ass Stuart, that's a good name. Take my advice Stuart—go in there and ask for Shelly. Tell her I sent you and tell her that I send my love."

How could I say no to that? I knew that if this guy Mike said the Brown Jug was the best bar in the world, it had to be a pretty fucking strange place. I almost felt like it was my civic duty to go check it out. Kenny and I settled our tab, said good-bye and thanks to our new friends, and set out for Shelly and the Brown Jug.

My first impression of the Brown Jug was that it looked the way that redneck biker bars always look in movies. There were framed posters of motorcycles on the wall, and a neon Budweiser light that kept trying to end its miserable life and finally flicker out for good. But here's how we knew we were getting into some weird shit; instead of playing the expected music, like Lynyrd Sky-nyrd or David Allen Coe, the jukebox was blaring mid-80's adult

contemporary light rock, like Level 42 or Hiroshima. A bit confused and caught off guard, we sat down at the bar and prepared
to order some drinks.

I addressed the bartender who was drying some glasses behind the bar.

"Hi, are you Shelly?"

She eyed me suspiciously and said hesitantly, "Yeah."

"Cool," I said, "We just came from Jonell's where we met
Mike. He's a really nice guy. He told me to tell you 'hi' and that
he sends his love." At this she shook her head, chortled a bit
and walked away to grab some more glasses. Now I was really
confused and felt a little uneasy. She came back and I tried once
more, "Mike's your husband right? He's the one who told us about
this place. He said it was the best bar in the world."

Shelly put down the glass she was working on and spit out
her reply, "I don't talk to that motherfucker when he's been drinking. Shit, I don't even talk to that motherfucker when he's been
thinking about drinking, that rotten piece of shit." Um ... *awk-
ward!* Shelly then picked up the glass again, took a breath and
said, "Now what the fuck can I get you?"

"Two Budweisers," Kenny answered. I was really glad not
to be talking to Shelly anymore. She brought over the beers and
Kenny paid her while I did my best not to look him in the eye for
fear that I would lose my shit and burst into hysterical laughter.
I turned to my right and saw at the end of the bar a lady looking like a washed up, drunk as hell, Diana Ross making weird
scrunched up faces at her drink. She and I made eye contact, so I
waved to her and said, "Hello." She replied by giving me the finger. She continued to do so every time I looked over there for the
rest of the night.

I turned to Kenny, holding back a giggle, and said, "You can't
win 'em all," and then pulled out my notebook and began writing
a few notes.

Meanwhile, Kenny somehow befriended the lost Supreme. I
overheard him ask her, "So why don't you like my friend?"

"Cuz he's white! That's why! You're alright cuz ... what are

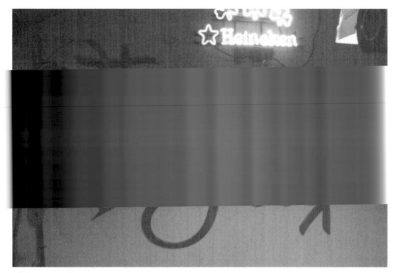

This is just a teaser photo of the Brown Jug. If I showed you any other photos of the place I might ruin its...uh...magic.

you Chinese or something?" she asked.

"Uh, Taiwanese," he said.

She cut him off and mumbled, "Yeah, cuz you're Chinese or something. But he's white! Waving at me and smiling and shit." At this point I looked over at them from my notebook and was once again met by her middle finger.

"Fuck it," I thought, and turned to my left where I saw a crumpled up old man who looked like he'd been sitting on the same barstool every night since 1948. I smiled at him and nodded, but got no response. Just as I was about to return to my notebook, some cheesy song that only gets airplay on your mom's love-song stations, like "I Go Crazy (Each Time that I Look in Your Eyes)" came on (okay so I secretly love that song, but don't tell anyone). The old guy next to me suddenly got all animated and started silently waving his cigarette around in the air and grinning like someone who just had their first taste of baby flesh and realized that they loved it. This was the point when I realized that the Brown Jug probably *was* the best bar in the world, but that it was far too much for my fragile soul to handle. It was like having your mind opened up to all the secrets of the universe and realizing that maybe you didn't want to know those secrets after all. I gathered Kenny and we walked out the door.

* * *

"That was *amazing*," Kenny said as we were walking down Hyde towards Market Street.

"Dude, I know. I seriously can't wait to write about that shit. Like, I really gotta hand it to Mike; I think that old blowhard was right about the Brown Jug," I answered.

"Yeah, but I've got the feeling that the reason he thinks it's the 'Best Bar in the World' and the reason we do might be at odds with each other."

"You're probably right, but goddamn, I'm still really blown away." By this point we'd had a good five or six drinks, and my stomach was telling me it was time to put some food in it. Call it the drunk munchies if you want. We were approaching Market. "Hey man, you hungry?" I asked Kenny.

"Yeah, I could eat. What's open?"

"Lemme think ... *oh! yes! yes!* Carl's Jr. at like 7th is open! Dude, have you ever had a Western Bacon Cheeseburger?"

"Nah man, I don't really eat fast food," Kenny said as we turned on to Market and I started leading us to the Promised Land of curly fries and milkshakes.

"It's not fast food! It's the fucking Western Bacon Cheese-burger! It's like in the upper echelon of man's achievements, with like, fire and space flight!" Kenny laughed, but I continued. "I'm not fucking joking. This is serious; we're going. You don't have to have one, but I sure as hell am."

We went to Carl's Jr. where we both sat and ate our delicious Western Bacon Cheeseburgers amidst the homeless and the fluo-rescent lights and the rancor and the stench that is Market Street at 2 a.m. I was satiated, and it had been a good night. I was ready to go home. Kenny and I walked out of Carl's Jr. and grabbed the first cab we saw.

The cabbie looked to be about our age and he had a thick accent that sounded like he had grown up in a former Soviet republic like Russia, or possibly the Ukraine. Since he was driving one of those nice new cabs that Desoto ~~always~~ ~~...~~ ~~...~~

~~...g ... tai tiic lyrics—~~ How do you *vant* it? How do you *feeel*? *Comeen* up as a *neeggah* in *dat* cash game, *Leevin* in *dat* fast lane, I'm for *reeel*!" The rest of the short ride consisted of the cab driver playing his favorite Tupac songs for us while he and Kenny discussed their theories about why Pac really wasn't actually dead. I was fucked up enough that I couldn't even tell if Kenny seriously thought Tupac was alive or if he was just egging this guy on.

We finally got dropped off in the Mission. Kenny lit his last cigarette contemplatively and said, "So, what a boring night, huh?"

I went along with it, "Yeah, nothing interesting ever happens to us."

"Did you at least get some good stuff for the book?"

"Nah, I think under the Tenderloin section I'll just put 'BOR-ING' in big letters and leave the rest blank." We laughed at ourselves. "Thanks for coming out tonight man, it was a lot of fun."

"Yes it was. I'm glad we did it. You'll have to let me know when the next research trip is, I'm totally down to go."

"Cool. I'm doing the Marina sometime this week."
"The Marina? Um...," Kenny blew out a puff of smoke, "scratch what I just said. You're on your own for the Marina."

"Fair enough," I said and then we did the whole handshake/man-hug thing and I went home and passed the fuck out. **S**

Market & SOMA

Market is *the* main street in downtown San Francisco and because of this it has different characteristics at different parts along its length. Market between Embarcadero and 5th is considered part of the Financial District and is primarily a place of commerce for people who dress nice and make a lot of money. Market between 5th and Van Ness is a place of commerce as well, but is pretty fucking Tenderloin-ish to say the least. Market from Van Ness on is not entirely, but mostly, the Castro. The part we are currently concerned with is that special little stretch between 5th and Van Ness. This is an area replete with titty bars, "urban athletic clothing stores", crackheads, homeless people, hard-working immigrant storeowners and weird ass knick-knack shops. In terms of shopping, you can find anything down here and every price is negotiable.

SOMA (South of Market) was formerly an industrial zone that got revamped and revitalized during the dot-com boom of the 1990s. Since that time it has been a haven for art galleries, expensive restaurants, expensive clubs, computer companies and of course, homeless people. The most happening part of SOMA is definitely the area around 11th Street and Folsom, but really there are cool little things scattered all over.

Food

This is a power-lunch-with-the-boss's-secretary-who-you're-try-ing-to-fuck type of place. It's got that corporate clean feel akin to a Panda Express, but it's not as streamlined. The prices are pretty good, meaning that for under $6 you can get very full. And best of all, they have Mitchell's Ice Cream. I love ice cream.

City's Choice
301 5th St. @ Folsom St.

This is just your basic no frills, inexpensive deli and liquor store. The people who work there are nice and the food is decent. That's all I'm gonna say about that.

Costco
450 10th St. @ Harrison St.

Find a friend with a Costco card. Go to Costco. Eat as many sam-ples as you want. Go home satisfied. Repeat.

Crêpes a Go-Go
350 11th St. @ Folsom St.

If you happen to be down in the 11th and Folsom area drinking or seeing a show, come last call, you are probably gonna want to put something in your belly. Well, Crêpes a Go-Go is the place for you. To begin with, the crêpes start at $3, making them very affordable, and they are bigger than a lot of crêpes I've seen in other parts of the city. This is also a great place to make your last valiant effort at getting laid because so many people from the surrounding bars come here before going home.

Latte Express
48 5th St. @ Jesse St.

Your basic no frills sandwich shop where you can get a decent bite for under $5. It's had a facelift since the days when I worked as an intern at a nearby office. It looks a lot healthier. Besides sandwiches, they also sell donuts and those boba tapioca ball drinks.

Market & 6th Food Corner
Market St. @ 6th St.

This place is, uh ... unique. They have all sorts of food, from Hofbrau to Chinese, and it is super cheap. For example, you can get two hot cakes, two strips of bacon and one egg for $3.50 plus tax, or any variation of a three-egg omelet for $4.25. But as I said this place is, uh ... unique. The patrons are the dregs of Market Street—the bottom of the barrel. I've seen numerous people get kicked out yelling and screaming, and I just keep my eyes on my grilled ham and cheese sandwich. But fuck it, it's really cheap.

Oriental Restaurant
1107 Market St. @ 7th St.

Definitely one of the cheapest places I have ever seen, but I cannot personally vouch for the food itself. A small plate (which is probably big enough to fill you up) is only $1.75. Egg rolls are only $0.85 and potstickers are only $0.65. And to top it all off, a beer is only $1.95. If you've got an iron stomach and an empty wallet, this is the place for you.

Rainbow Pizza
1083 Market St. @ McAllister St.

A tiny little pizza joint in the middle of Market Street. You can get a small sub sandwich for $3.99, and a small Calzone for only $5. Pretty decent prices for a pretty decent place. I like calzones; I like them a lot.

Red's Java House
Embarcadero between Piers 30-32

Someone just got a beer and a burger for less than $6. You can't even get syphilis that cheap these days.

I just recently found this place and I absolutely love it. Red's is basically a little shack between two piers on the Embarcadero that has been selling good cheap meals since 1918. You can get a double cheeseburger and a beer for $5.60. The best part about Red's though, is that it has a great back patio that's practically on the water. The patio has a full bar, which accommodates a diverse clientele ranging from bikers to businessmen.

Ted's Market
1530 Howard St. @ 11ᵗʰ St.

Despite initially seeming like a typical liquor and deli, Ted's is actually the secret headquarters for the San Francisco chapter of the CIA. Well, not really, but they do make sandwiches that are big, fresh, delicious and mostly under $5. Their sandwiches are big enough to be two meals if you are someone my size or smaller, and big enough to make a larger person very full.

Tu Lan

8 6ᵗʰ St. @ Market St.

A veritable broke-ass San Francisco institution, Tu Lan has been serving good, cheap Vietnamese food since long before I set foot in the City. Motherfuckers *love* this place. Maybe it's because the food here comes in heaping portions and everything on the menu costs between $4.50 and $7.50; or it's because meat eaters and vegetarians have almost an equal amount of choices. The food comes out quickly, the place is always busy, and the staff couldn't give a fuck about being polite to you. Sounds like heaven, right?

Bars

...most is that the drinks are well priced. When you walk in it appears to be just like any other narrow dive bar, but when you get to the back you realize, "Holy shit! This looks like a cave!" Unlike most caves though, this one is usually packed tight with a bunch of hipsters dancing poorly to bad 80's music. (Why has bad 80's music become cool again? What the fuck?) The best thing about this bar though is that on Sunday nights, well drinks and cans of Pabst are only $1. I'll brave bad music for drinks that cheap any day.

Butter
354 11th St. @ Folsom St.

I've been to plenty of bars all over the United States whose clientele happen to be kinda white trash, but only in San Francisco can you find a bar that actually has a white trash theme. This bar is Butter. The interior has velvet Elvis paintings, the beers of choice are Pabst Blue Ribbon and Budweiser and you can even order your favorite "trailer-trash" type of food. The funny thing about the bar is that there are never any actual white trash people inside, but if you ever feel like seeing how the other half lives, stop in at Butter.

The City Beer Store and Tasting Room
1168 Folsom St. between 7th St. & 8th St.

Kinda like a wine bar but for beer drinkers, City Beer serves as a place to learn about really good beer and then buy it by the pint, bottle or six-pack. Basically the way it works is, you go in and pick a beer from the fridge or one on tap, and then you drink it. If you've got any questions or want suggestions, homeboy behind the bar knows more about beer than I know about anything. If you buy a bottle or sixer, you can take it home with you, and if you wanna drink it there, there's a small corkage fee. It's truly a brilliant idea; my only comment is that it lacks a little ambience, like at least get a Lava-lamp or something. But my guess is that the beer snobs that are coming from all over the city probably don't give a shit about ambience. Word to the wise: this spot closes at 9 p.m. from Tuesday through Saturday and 6 p.m. on Sunday. It's closed on Monday.

The Eagle Tavern
398 12th St. @ Harrison St.

This SOMA bar is one of the most mixed in the city. Gay, straight, biker, punk, etc. can all be found at this cool, little dive bar. They also have one of the most belly-filling happy hours around. On Sundays between 3 and 6 p.m., you pay just $10 for all the beer you can drink. Not too shabby, hey pal?

Eddie Rickenbacker's
133 2nd St. @ Mission St.

Apparently there was a time in U.S. history where at most bars, happy hour meant cheap drinks *and* free food. Or so my Pops tells me. Unfortunately, that time is not now. But never fear, dear readers, I have done my best to find you the few that do exist in SF, and Eddie Rickenbacker's is one of them. Stop in between 5 and 7 p.m., buy a drink and just wait for the appetizers to roll out. When I was there yesterday, the waitress brought out a small, delicious piece of steak and an awesome buffalo wing. The bad part was that they came out 30 minutes apart. The good part is that they have a vat of gnarly-ass cheese and a basket of crackers to sustain you in between. They also have beautiful antique motorcycles (some from around the turn of the century) all over the place and authentic guns in an Indian Fighter display (which some people might find pretty tasteless).

Maya

..., and out of all of them, Maya's is one of the best tasting, and easily the best displayed. The happy hour runs from 5 to 7 p.m., Monday through Friday; and if tequila is your thing, Maya has a bazillion different kinds you can try.

The Stud

399 9th St. @ Harrison St.

Having been a Queer establishment since 1966 (way before the term Queer was reclaimed as a positive word), The Stud has managed to assert itself as one of the best gay spots in the whole City. On most nights it's a chill place to hang out, play some pool and have some drinks, but don't let those nights fool you because, come Tuesday, The Stud comes alive with Trannyshack, the wildest, best and most famous Drag Night in the Bay Area. If your cousins from Idaho are visiting for the week, and you really want to blow their feeble minds, then Trannyshack is just what they need.

Shopping

Beyond Beads
1251 Howard St. @ 8th St.

A lot of my more crafty friends rave about how great this bead store is. Me, I'm not so crafty, so it seems like just another store full of beads, but apparently they have some of the best prices around, and the staff is really helpful. If you go there let me know how it is, and make me a bracelet while you're at it. Thanks.

The San Francisco Chocolate Factory
286 12th St. @ Folsom St.

Don't get your hopes up. There's no eccentric and snarky candy millionaire running around with a platoon of orange-faced, musical midgets, drowning fat kids in rivers of chocolate and belittling the elderly. No ma'am, not here—that's called heaven. Despite that one major shortcoming though, the San Francisco Chocolate Factory is a great place because they do one thing really well: they make delicious chocolate. Considering that these chocolates are a bit of a luxury item, they're fairly well priced; yummy goodness starts at just $0.99. And they have this whole system where you can buy your goodies by the percent of cocoa in them. White chocolate is 31 percent, milk chocolate is 38 percent and the dark stuff ranges from 55 percent to 72 percent. Personally, I'm a 38 percenter.

P.S. I miss Gene Wilder.

SF Flower Mart
640 Brannan St. @ 6ᵗʰ St.

Okay, so you really fucked up this time. Not only did you forget

you are going into the flower shop business, make sure to stop in at the office so that you can get your retailer's badge. You gotta be legit in the flower shop game, sucka!

United Nations Plaza Bazaar
Market St. @ 9ᵗʰ St.

Every Monday, Thursday and Friday a bazaar of sorts is held at United Nations Plaza. This is a great place to get things like incense, bootlegged videos, hunting knives, Garbage Pail Kids stickers, and cheap exotic looking jewelry for yourself or your significant other. Remember just about everything is up for negotiation, so it's easy to walk away with some cool crap for pretty cheap.

Sights & Entertainment

Bamboo Garden
560 Mission St.

Right next to the big business building at 560 Mission is a tiny little bamboo garden. This serene little place is a nice haven from the hecticness that is downtown San Francisco. Besides bamboo, there is a cool fountain/sculpture that has small little stepping stones. If you're walking on these, and someone is looking at you from the street, it appears that you're walking on water. Looks like Jesus isn't the only Jewish kid in town who knows that trick. Now if I could only turn water into Budweiser ...

Brainwash Café
1122 Folsom St. @ 8th St.

www.brainwash.com

The Brainwash is probably the coolest laundromat in the entire universe. Not only is it a place that allows you to wash your clothes, it is also a place that allows you to eat food, drink beer and see performances. Whether it's a singer-songwriter showcase or a DJ line-up, the Brainwash has something interesting going on almost every night of the week. This being said, it is not the cheapest place in the city to eat, or wash your clothes; but if nothing else, it's probably the most entertaining. And they have pretty good prices on beer: most domestics are $2.50 and during happy hour Pabst is only a buck. Be sure to check out their Thursday night comedy open-mic which is hosted by a very funny man named Tony.

California Academy of the Sciences
875 Howard St. @ 5th St.

While its usual home in Golden Gate Park is being completely
redone, this...

California Historical Society
678 Mission St. @ 3rd St.

Truthfully, I was a little let down by this place. It is pretty small
and really didn't have that much in it. Luckily it's only $3 to get in,
or $1 if you have a student ID. The exhibits are always changing
so sometimes the museum is more interesting than others.

The Cartoon Art Museum
@ Yerba Buena Gardens

Started more than 15 years ago with an endowment from *Peanuts*
creator Charles Schulz, the Cartoon Art Museum is the only one
of its kind in the U.S. This museum is exactly what the name
implies, showcasing the likes of Dr. Seuss and Charles Schulz,
among others. The entrance fee is normally just $6, but on the
first Tuesday of every month they have a "pay what you can" day.

Defenestration Building
214 6th St. @ Howard St.

To defenestrate is to throw something or somebody out of a window. It is actually a word (my spell checker didn't even underline
it with the squiggly red line) and artist Brian Goggin demon-
strated its meaning by attaching tons of furniture to the outside of
this building. Although it looks more like they're trying to escape
something inside rather than actually being thrown from a win-

Somebody in China just got poked by the other end of that arrow.

dow, it's still a fantastic art piece to check out if you don't mind standing at one of the shittiest corners in San Francisco.

The Embarcadero

..... ~~~p~~, ~~~ ~~~~ you have found! What a perfect place to start a settlement where Missionaries can come to convert and torture Natives. Well done Señor!" Walking along the Embarcadero is a magnificent way to kill an afternoon.

The Metreon
4th St. @ Mission St.

Located at 4th and Mission, the Metreon is, amongst other things, a very expensive movie theater. But it also has one of the coolest things *ever!!* Inside they have a Sony Playstation room full of Playstations where you can just sit and play until they kick you out. Sometimes they expect you to give up the controller after ten minutes, but other times they let you play longer. It's a great way to entertain yourself for free.

Museum of the African Diaspora
685 Mission St. @ 3rd St.

This relatively new museum largely focuses on the history and heritage of all those in the Americas who are of African descent. The building is all sleek and high-concept design and the exhibitions are fascinating. Unfortunately though, I don't think they have a free days, so if you wanna go, you'll have to cough up $10 or $5 if you're old or have a student ID.

SFMOMA
151 3rd St. @ Howard St.

The San Francisco Museum of Modern Art is truly world class. It's got all the heavy hitters of modern art like Jackson Pollock, Pablo Picasso, Diego Rivera, Frida Kahlo and Andy Warhol. (You know what's interesting? Out of all the artists just mentioned, Microsoft Word only put the squiggly red line under the words "Frida Kahlo". How sexist is that?) It's also located within a building as architecturally impressive as the collection inside. One of the things the museum is most noted for is its collection of pop art. It's really a shame to be in SF and not see this museum, so I recommend going on the first Tuesday of the month, when it's free. Alternatively you can go on Thursday evenings from 6 to 9 p.m. and only pay $6. Otherwise it's $12.50.

Slim's
333 11th St. @ Folsom St.

www.slims-sf.com

Founded by Boz Skaggs, Slim's has been one of the best live music venues in the City since it first opened in 1988. Considering the caliber of performers (George Clinton, Dinosaur Jr., NOFX, Rakim, etc.,) the ticket prices are fairly reasonable. Let's not lie to ourselves, it is a venue with big name bands, so tickets aren't dirt cheap, but they are cheaper than anything you'll pay at the Fillmore.

Yerba Buena Gardens
Mission St. @ 4th St.

Practically connected to the Metreon is Yerba Buena Gardens. Although it is not huge, it does have a nice flower garden and a cool little waterfall/pond thingy. It's a great place to lay in the sun and read a book if you are tired of busy downtown.

Cool # Architecture
$12.50 → $6 ^{Thursday} 6-9

FREE → 1st tuesdays

POP ART → Warhol

SOMA

GRUB-A-DUB-DUB

1 Asia Chinese Food
2 City's Choice
3 Costco
4 Latte Express
5 Market & 6th Food
   Corner
6 Oriental Restaurant
7 OSHA Thai Noodle
   House
8 Rainbow Pizza
9 Red's Java House
10 Ted's Market
11 Tu Lan

FREE FOOD!

12 Eddie Rickenbacker's
13 Maya
14 The Tempest

LATE NITE EATS

15 Crepes-A-Go-Go
16 Denny's
16.5 Happy Donuts
17 Mel's Drive-In

DRINKS DRINKS DRINKS

18 Arrow Bar
19 Butter
20 The City Beer Store
   & Tasting Room
21 The Eagle Tavern
22 The Stud

PLACES TO CHECK OUT

23 Bamboo Garden
24 Brainwash Cafe
25 California Historical
   Society
26 The Cartoon Art Museum
27 The Embarcadero
28 The Metreon
29 Yerba Buena Gardens
30 Museum Of The
   African Diaspora
31 SF MOMA
32 CA Academy of the
   Sciences
33 Slim's

The Richmond

Back in the nineteenth century, very few people lived in the Richmond. Sure there were plenty of people out there, but none of them were alive. That's because up until the early twentieth century, the Richmond was made up of primarily two things: sand dunes and cemeteries. Then in the 30's, all of the cemeteries in the City were moved to what is now Colma. Around the same time, the streetcar finally made it out to the Richmond, thus opening it up for people to move there and build actual houses for their families instead of just living in apartment buildings. By the middle of the last century, waves of immigrants were coming to San Francisco. It was during this time that the Richmond District became the unofficial home for sizable Irish and Russian populations. These days, the Richmond is considered a sort of second Chinatown because of the huge Chinese population and the semi-recent influx of South East Asians, making Clement Street one of the most interesting eating/shopping areas this side of the Pacific Ocean. Clement is chock full of some of the best, cheapest and most diverse restaurants that the City has to offer. It's also packed with stores in which you can find anything imaginable needed for daily life. It was actually kinda hard to pick places to write about because so much of the Richmond would fit perfectly in this guide. And just so you know, the Richmond District is pretty much the area west of Masonic/Presidio, north of Golden Gate Park, and south of the Presidio.

Food

fish and organic chicken. This means that all the meat was raised free range, on a veggie diet, and without hormones. Because the meat was raised so ethically, it is a smidgen more expensive than meat at other places, but really, it's only a smidgen. The sandwiches that you buy here are huge and the most expensive one is $6.29. They also have an AK Subs at Harrison and 8th St. that has more food choices, but doesn't sell the meat in bulk like the Clement location.

Bazaar Café

5927 California St. @ 21st Ave.

www.bazaarcafe.com

Oooh, I really like this place. It has all the basic prerequisites of a great café, like free WiFi, comfy seats and good food and drinks. But then it goes a few steps further. The café has a fantastic backyard garden/patio and excellent art on consignment lining the walls (ahem, that was a hint for all you artists to try to get your shit in there so maybe you can sell some pieces). And then to make it even cooler, it has live performances every night ranging from open mics to storytelling to an Art and Politics night hosted by Matt Gonzalez (if you don't know who he is, you should Google him or something). The Bazaar also has a listening station where you can hear music by some of the café's performers and purchase their music. I really, really like this place.

Bok Choy Garden
1820 Clement St. @ 19th Ave.

Back in the day, San Francisco must have had a ludicrous amount
of diners. I don't know how many places I've been to that are
laid out like old school diners but are now Mexican or Asian
food joints. Bok Choy Garden is one of these. What used to be a
diner (it still has the wood panel walls and the flower patterned
tablecloths) is now an extremely well-priced vegetarian Chinese
food restaurant. The most expensive thing here is $7.50, and most
dishes are around six bucks.

D&A Café
407 Clement St. @ 5th Ave.

Clement St. is full of Asian restaurants, some less expensive than
others. If you're reading this, you are probably looking for something cheap. At the D&A Café, you can get very full for fewer than
eight bucks. Most everything on the menu is super inexpensive,
but if you are looking for the biggest bang for your buck, go for
one of their set meals. I got a teriyaki chicken steak, soup, rice
and a Coke for $6.50. They also have lunch meals for something
ridiculous like $3.80. Also, they're open until 1 a.m., in case you
wander out of one of the surrounding pubs looking for grub.

Eats
50 Clement St. @ 2nd Ave.

Eats is neither the cheapest nor the best greasy spoon breakfast
place in the City, but on the other hand, it's not too expensive or
that bad. What can I say? It's a bit of an ambiguous place. Most of
the food is under $5.95, and the ladies who work there are very
nice. The end.

Haig's Delicacies
642 Clement St. @ 8th Ave.

Haig's has been selling imported packaged food and spices in the
same spot for over 40 years. The goods are mostly from India and

the Middle East. This is a great place to shop if you are looking for those hard to find spices. For those of you who are as impatient as I am with regards to cooking, Haig's also has a deli where you can get hot food to go.

...y .... burgers are under $6 and you can get a big-ass breakfast for $3.99.

King of Thai Noodle
639 Clement St. @ 7th Ave.

(see entry on page 174)

Lucky Penny
2670 Geary Blvd. @ Masonic Ave.

I always think of this place as Denny's semi-retarded little brother. The food is completely mediocre, but cheap. It also happens to be the only 24-hour place in the near vicinity to my knowledge. The interior reminds me of all the little truck-stop diners off the free-way in the middle of butt-fuck, nowhere, throughout the United States. All I can really say about this place is that it's pretty cheap, and don't get the steak.

Minh's Garden
208 Clement St. @ 3rd Ave.

The tag line on the window outside said, "Experience Authentic Vietnamese Cuisine Fresh Good and Inexpensive". It was almost as if that tricky bastard Minh knew my weak spot. So I stopped in for lunch. Minh was right.

Pho Tu Do

1000 Clement St. @ 11th Ave.

The pho (a Vietnamese noodle soup) here is amazing and it comes in a bowl big enough for Shaquille O'Neal to soak his feet in. It's like three meal's worth for $6.50. The rest of the menu is also really good too. My favorite thing about this place used to be the wallpaper that was supposed to make you feel like you were in a bamboo forest, but now they've updated the look of the place. Bummer.

Pizza Orgasmica

823 Clement St. @ 9th Ave;
also at 3157 Fillmore St. @ Greenwich St.

Between the name of the place and pizzas called Doggie Style and Ménage à Trois, it's pretty easy to figure out what the theme is here. What I haven't quite put my finger on is what the theme is for this renowned Richmond pizzeria's interior. It's got kind of a King-Arthur's-Court-meets-India-meets-Africa thing going on. All that aside, the pizza is really good, they brew their own beer and they have really stellar nightly drink specials. To name a few, Thursday night has $2.50 pints of Guinness and free pizza bites, while Saturday (80's night), has $3.50 Long Island Iced Teas. The Marina location still has good pizza but unfortunately not any of the funky character.

Bars

This is an interactive photo. Go grab a beer, open it, "clank" your bottle against mine and say "Cheers!" If you really just did that, you have a serious drinking problem and should seek help. Photo by Trisha Gum

pubs and the late-night Vietnamese restaurants that make up the Richmond's night life is the 540 Club, a genuine, bona fide dive bar. The vibe of the place makes you wonder why it's not in the Mission, but then you realize how little you are paying for your strong drink, and decide that you don't care where it is. Monday nights here are ridiculous—$1 well drinks—and Tuesdays are almost as crazy because well drinks are $2. But the art on the walls and the jukebox and/or DJ make it a nice place to hang out any night of the week.

The Dog's Bollix
408 Clement St. @ 5th Ave.

I don't know what it's normally like, but I walked in here right after smoking a bowl and just before last call to find "Don't Stop Believing" by Journey blaring over the speakers. It was such complete and utter mayhem that the truthfulness of anything else I might say would be compromised.

Ireland's 32
3920 Geary Blvd. @ 3rd Ave.

Stepping into this bar, you have no doubts as to what the owner's sentiments are regarding The Troubles in Northern Ireland. There are Sinn Fein (the legal and political arm of the IRA) posters everywhere and painted portraits of Bobby Sands and Gerry Adams. But you know what's funny? The owner is actually an American who is just fascinated by Northern Ireland. If I walked into this bar in Belfast, I'd be fucking terrified because it would be an IRA bar, but luckily, in SF it's just a place to see live music and drink. The drinks aren't super cheap, but it really does feel like a proper Irish pub and even has pub grub and a second floor with pool tables and darts.

O'Keefe's Bar
598 5th Ave. @ Balboa St.

This place is super neighborhoody. When we walked in, everyone in the joint stared at us; not in a menacing way, but in a way that said, "Who the fuck are these people and how on earth did they end up in here?" The drinks here are *strong* (like you have to be careful not to puke after the first sip) and *cheap* (a 7&7 is only four bucks). We must have been served by Annie (the sign outside says, "Annie & Tim" under "O'Keefe's"), who was fairly surly; she was far more interested in chatting with regulars than serving us. When my girlfriend asked for a lime for her VODKA soda (get it?), Annie reached over the bar and actually squeezed the lime into the drink herself (I know it doesn't sound weird, but it looked it). You can smoke inside, which is the reason we only had one drink here; that and the fact that one drink was enough to give us a buzz.

The Plough and Stars
116 Clement St. @ 2nd Ave.

It never ceases to amaze me that, no matter where you go in the world, you can find an Irish pub. I've been to one as far out as

Prague, and it was absolutely bananas with motherfuckers dancing on tables and throwing coasters around the room as if they were Frisbees. Having spent quite a bit of time in Ireland, I can testify to the fact that this is a pretty authentic place. I mean f~

~~ ~~~~~ ~~ ~~~~ was the semi-famous Last Day Saloon ... proverbially of course. Actually the Last Day Saloon closed and the Rockit Room opened up in the same space, so there really was no ash-rising at all, but it certainly sounds more romantic that way, doesn't it? The Rockit Room is the best place in the Richmond to see up-and-coming local and touring acts. They get everything from bluegrass to Riot Grrrl punk. Another good thing about the joint is that you can drink, shoot pool, play foosball and watch sports downstairs, without having to pay to go upstairs for the show.

Trad'r Sam's
6150 Geary Blvd. @ 26th Ave.

Every once in a while you come across a bar that people will flock to from all over the City. Often it's some brand new hot spot where drinks are $11, the doorman is a monstrosity, and there is a line around the block to get in. Trad'r Sam's is none of these. It has been a favorite of San Franciscans ever since it first opened in 1939. The doorperson is friendly and just wants to see an ID, and the only abnormally priced drinks are the ones for four people that come in bowls. The only drawback of this old-school Tiki lounge is that it gets really packed on weekends and the crowd can be kind of bro-ish if you know what I mean.

Shopping

Cheaper than Cheaper

Clement between 8th & 9th Aves.

This place is really no different than any of the other cheap goods stores found all over the Richmond, Mission and China-town. But given the name, I couldn't resist putting it in the book. Here you can get all sorts of stupidly cheap household goods. Quality is by no means guaranteed.

Green Apple Books & Music

506 Clement St. @ 6th Ave.

If you are in the Richmond District and want to spend a day just dicking around, then go to Green Apple. This is one of the best

bookstores in the entire city because they have a fantastic selection of new and used books and music as well as a considerable amount of periodicals. I actually found back issues of *Midwifery Today* maga-zine, no bullshit. My only complaint about Green Apple is that its new CDs are kinda pricey, but hey, what can you do? So go out and support this lovely local business.

After seeing this sign, I spent 45 minutes looking for a glory hole before realizing it was advertising cheap books about sex. Damn you Green Apple, you tricky bastards!!!

The Hobby Company of San Francisco

5150 Geary Blvd. @ 16th Ave.

Too cool to spend your leisure time playing video games, lurking
on myspace, or doing d--- º D

. ... been described as crafty, so
don't expect to see me hanging out there.

San Francisco Brewcraft

1555 Clement St. @ 17th Ave.

www.sfbrewcraft.com

So you wanna be a beer brewer? At SF Brewcraft you get all the
gear you need and the ingredients to brew five gallons of the beer
of your choice, plus a free step-by-step brewing class all for $94.
Sweet, right? Plus, you get to go in and hang out with Griz, a titan
of a man who rocks a big white beard and denim overalls. Just
imagine if Santa Claus rode a Harley and lived in the Santa Cruz
Mountains, brewing beer, dropping acid and chopping his own
wood and shit. Griz kinda looks like that, but much cooler.

Sights & Entertainment

Park Life
220 Clement St. @ 3rd Ave.

Although they do sell stuff here like music, art and neat books about music and art, the stuff here isn't exactly cheap, so I decided to put it in the Sights/Entertainment section. This actual store is a bit of an anomaly out here in the Richmond; it seems like it belongs in the Haight or Mission, but that's one of the things that makes it so cool. Another is that they get really great art exhibits. For example, this one time I went in and they had a whole exhibit of music photography. This one particular piece was amazing—12 or so Polaroids from some party in the late 70's; amongst the photos of various punks there was one of Sid Vicious and another one of Iggy Pop. It was like opening up a pack of baseball cards and getting a Tony Gwynn rookie card.

The Legion of Honor
Lincoln Park, 34th Ave. @ Clement St.

Although this museum is way the fuck out there, it's completely worth the trek. Why? I'm so glad you asked. The view of the ocean and the Golden Gate Bridge (if I remember right) is beautiful, and the building housing the museum is as exquisite as the art inside. The museum was built with money from all kinds of railroad baron types (who were probably trying to expunge their consciences of past evils), to look like a building in Paris called the Palais de la Legion d'Honneur, which is French for, "Museum that's way the fuck out there". This museum is free every Tuesday, and on all other days you get $2 off by showing your Muni pass or transfer.

The San Francisco Columbarium

1 Loraine Ct. (1 block west of Stanyan) @ Anza St.

Back before the turn of the twentieth century, cemeteries took up most of the Richmond. A 1901 law ~~~ ~
d~~~ ~ ~

...........cent of the Duomo
~~~~~. When you go, make sure to ask for Emmitt Watson, the caretaker. He's been there for years and knows all about the place's history. One funny thing that I noticed was that the mail box said "No. One Loraine Court", but since the dot is faded, it looks like "No One", which is kinda funny considering that, literally, no one lives there.

Sutro Baths/Cliff House/Camera Obscura

1090 Point Lobos Ave. @ The Great Highway

There's a lot of history I could put in here, but I'm gonna try to make this as quick as possible because otherwise I would end up with a book report (as well as a plagiarism lawsuit). First of all, I'm not actually sure if this is still technically in the Richmond but since I don't really give a fuck, the Richmond it will be.

Sutro Baths: These are actually nothing more than the ruins of what was once a huge three-acre complex filled with seven different public baths, built around the turn of the century by millionaire Adolph Sutro. It was an ice skating rink in the 30's, and now all that's left are ruins. You can walk around them and explore the nearby cave, which I haven't done, but I hear it's cool.

Cliff House: The Cliff House was a restaurant originally built in 1863 that was later gutted by fire in 1894. Then your boy Adolph Sutro spent a crazy amount of money and turned it into a gorgeous Victorian masterpiece, which was subsequently gutted by fire in 1907. I would *love* to put a photo of the Victorian version in here but, are you kidding me? It would be way too expensive to get the rights. Anyway, it was rebuilt in 1909 as basically a box with a little fringe at the top, and it still looks like that today. The restaurant inside is really expensive.

Camera Obscura: I've actually not been in here because it was closed when I went, but it's an SF landmark that's been around since 1946 when it was part of Playland on the Beach, an amusement park that no longer exists. The basic principal is that light is used to project live images of the surrounding ocean and beach onto the walls inside. It's supposed to be pretty cool, but all I got to see was the outside … bummer.

Ceci n'est pas une Giant Camera.

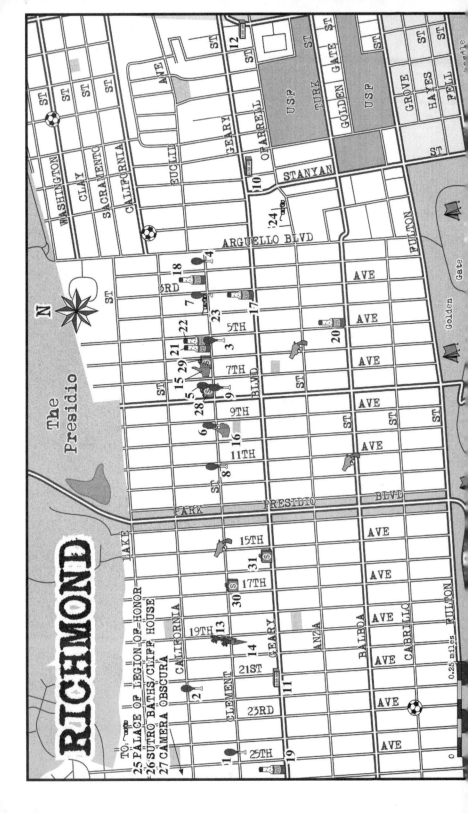

RICHMOND

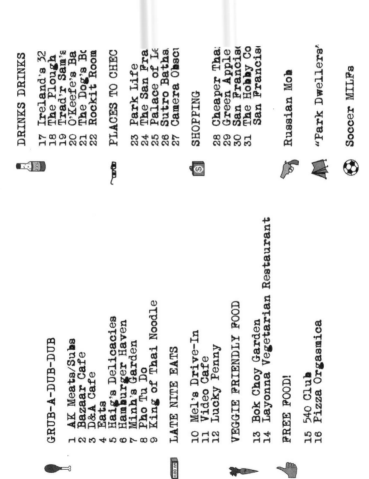

GRUB-A-DUB-DUB

1 AK Meats/Subs
2 Bazaar Cafe
3 D&A Cafe
4 Eats
5 Haig's Delicacies
6 Hamburger Haven
7 Minh's Garden
8 Pho Tu Do
9 King of Thai Noodle

LATE NITE EATS

10 Mel's Drive-In
11 Video Cafe
12 Lucky Penny

VEGGIE FRIENDLY FOOD

13 Bok Choy Garden
14 Layonna Vegetarian Restaurant

FREE FOOD!

15 540 Club
16 Pizza Orgasmica

DRINKS DRINKS

17 Ireland's 32
18 The Plough
19 Trad'r Sam's
20 O'Keefe's Ba
21 The Dog's Bc
22 Rockit Room

PLACES TO CHEC

23 Park Life
24 The San Fra
25 Palace of Le
26 Sutro Baths.
27 Camera Obsc

SHOPPING

28 Cheaper Tha:
29 Green Apple
30 San Francisc
31 The Hobby Co
    San Francisc

Russian Mob

"Park Dwellers'

Soccer MILFs

Broke-Ass Stuart's Basic Tips to Make Survival More Likely

Tipping: I can't stress how *important* it is to leave a good tip. For people who wait tables, tips are a major part of their income; and having been a server many times myself, I can't tell you how insulting it is when I work very hard to please someone only to receive a shitty tip. Here's a rough guide to tipping: tip your server 20%. How hard is that? I guess 18% is acceptable, but anything less sucks. Consider yourself a patron of the arts. Most of the servers I know only do it because it gives them enough freedom to pursue what they really want in life, so by tipping well you're helping artists, writers, actors and others creative people survive. How's this—if you think tipping 20% is too expensive, then just get your food to go and leave a couple bucks. Basically what I'm saying is that bad tippers shouldn't be allowed in restaurants. There, I'm glad I got that off my chest.

Sleeping: You're gonna have to go it alone on this one. What do you want me to do, write a review of your future apartment? I can't do everything. What I will do though is give you the resources so you can help yourself find a place to sleep. And worst comes to worst, there's always Golden Gate Park. If you're looking for an apartment, craigslist.org is really the only way to go. I've found every place I've ever lived in the City on craigslist. If you just plan on being here for a little while and want a decent hotel at a good price, try hotwire.com. My dad uses it every time he comes up here and he often gets shit like a four-star hotel for $80 a night. I'd imagine that two and three star places would be substantially cheaper. If you want to go a cheaper route and want to meet other people, try staying at one of San Francisco's 22 hostels. You can read about them and book online at hostelz.com. Anoth

Dumpster Diving: This is for those of you who spent your last pennies on this book. Dumpster diving is the practice of going through trashcans, generally from commercial businesses, and taking the things that were thrown away. As the old saying goes, "One man's trash is another man's treasure." A lot of my friends who dumpster dive do it in the dumpsters behind big markets like Safeway and smaller health food stores like Rainbow Grocery, where you can find a lot of edible produce. If you plan on diving, bring some bolt cutters in case those scoundrels lock their dumpsters.

Job Hunting: Because of San Francisco's size and the amount of people that seem to always be moving to it, finding a job can be fucking hard. Of course there's craigslist, but you're still competing with every other jobless chump out there. What I always suggest is this: pick a neighborhood and dress accordingly. If you're going to North Beach or the Marina, dress like you were going to your little cousin's bar mitzvah. If you're going to the Haight, dress like you did that one time when you tried out for *The Real World*. Bring out like 20 resumes a day and try to get rid of all of them. There will be a bunch of places that say, "Oh, we're not hiring but you can leave a résumé." If you like the place, leave one; I've been called like three months later—you just never know. Ya know?

Dolores Park Movie Night: What could be better than going to the park with cheap wine and cheap friends, and watching classic movies with 500 or so other revelers? Nothing. Every time I've gone to this, it ended up being a great night. This is how it works: on the second Thursday of each month, from April until October, a free movie is played on a giant screen in Dolores Park. Past movies have included *Charlie and the Chocolate Factory*, *Airplane*, and *Raiders of the Lost Ark*.

Open and Shut Locksmith (415) 504-KEYS: So I made a little deal with these guys, just for your benefit. The deal is that you can call 24 hours a day and tell them that you want the "Broke-Ass Stuart Special", and they will give you 15 percent off whatever work they do for you. All I had to do was promise my first-born child to them. Not a bad deal right? These guys are super good at their jobs and have 12 years of experience. Give them a ring.

Volunteer Ushering: Want to see a great show for free? Volunteer to be an usher. You can do this at the symphony, ACT, the opera, and even at the Fillmore and the Warfield. Contact the venue you're interested in to learn more about it.

Half-Price Theater Tickets: San Francisco has some really fantastic theater that comes through. If you want to go to a show, but don't want to pay tons of money, go to Tix in Union Square on the day of the show. Because the theater wants to get as many butts in seats as possible, they sell the remaining tickets for a show, day of, for half price. Theater, bitches! Who says I'm not highbrow?

1st Thursdays: The first Thursday of the month means art openings at the galleries in the Union Square area. Art openings mean free wine, cheese and other delectable edibles. If you wanna have some real fun, get totally wasted and start yelling things like, "You phonies know nothing about art! You wouldn't know a real artist if he came into your gallery drunk and started shouting things!" and then smash you wine glass on the floor and storm out. No, don't actually do that; you'd be such a dick if you did.

Food from Vendors at Street Festivals: After a street fair

drunken journey. But in retrospect, I think they were just trying to get a few final dollars.

Watch Your Step: Everybody has one true gift in this world. Some people are amazing athletes, while others are math geniuses. My true talent is stepping in dog shit. I am really amazing at it. If it were a vocation, I'd be a millionaire. So I've got an idea. You know how sometimes when a pet pees on the carpet, one way people punish them is to rub the animal's nose in it? I think that every dog owner who doesn't clean up after their animal when it shits in the street, should get their face rubbed in dog shit. That would teach those sons of bitches, right? Anyway, the moral of the story is that you should watch where you step because there is dog—and human—shit all over this city.

Food Court Discount: If you're in a food court, tell the cashier that you work in the mall. There is almost always a discount for people who work in the shopping center. This is true for most of the food courts I've ever been in.

Free Wine: A lot of the nice hotels downtown give out free wine from like 5 to7 p.m. every evening. Just go in and act like you're staying at the hotel. If for some reason a person asks you if you're actually staying there, just say something like, "No, but my uncle is, and I'm supposed to be meeting him here." Or something like that. Just use those improv skills that you learned in ninth-grade drama class.

Library Book Sales: On the first Friday of the month from April to October, you can buy books on the steps of the Main Library (100 Larkin St. @ Grove St.) for $1 each. If you're not actually gonna read the book, you can at least put it on your shelf so you look smart.

Speak Up: If you see someone attractive on the Muni or BART, don't be afraid to talk to them—something might come of it. I've met quite a few lovely women whilst in transit. In fact, don't be afraid to talk to most people on the Muni or BART. I always meet really interesting people riding public transit.

Free Smell Goods: I'm a cologne junkie; I just love the stuff. I'm not sure if people know this or not, but you can get perfume and cologne for free. Just go to a department store, pretend like you might want to buy some fragrances, and then ask them if they have some samples. They always do, and they will give you tiny take home bottles for free. So please *stop* smelling bad. This is the twenty-first century for fuck's sake. You know who you are.

Free Stuff: Has anyone but me ever noticed how many pairs of shoes are just lying around Haight Street? It's really unprecedented. This type of urban recycling is really one of the coolest things about the City. There is a lot of free stuff out there; you just have to be willing to take it with you (and probably wash it). You can find free clothes, shoes, furniture and especially books if you keep your eyes open. Don't be afraid—the worst you can get is scabies ... probably.

Camping: Did you know that you can go camping in San Francisco? I'm not talking about squatting in an abandoned house or sleeping in some bushes in Golden Gate Park, I mean sitting around a campfire, eating 'shrooms and making s'mores. There is a little known place in the Presidio called Rob Hill Campground where you can camp and get views of the Bay and the Pacific Ocean. Unfortunately, there are only two campsites and each of them is for 30 people. But if you can get together a group of people

˪ᴀᴍᴵ or Yellow Pages does. Here's the link:
http://sanfrancisco.zami.com/Thrift_Shop/A-Z

City Carshare/Zipcar/Flexcar: Owning a car here in the City can be such a fucking hassle. I had a car here for just one summer, and in that short time it got broken into, towed, and I got scores of parking tickets. The terms for each of these companies differ, but the basic premise is that you can rent a car for a short amount of time, and not have it cost you too much. The theory is that you get the convenience of having a car (the cars are parked all over the city for pick-up and drop-off) without spending all the money. Plus it's better for the environment than everyone driving their own cars all the time. Check out each one and see which you like best:
www.citycarshare.org; zipcar.com; flexcar.com.

Museums for FREE: San Francisco has some amazing museums—in fact, probably some of the best museums on the West Coast. Although normally, admission to these ranges from cheapo to expensive, most museums have a day at the beginning of every month where entrance is absolutely, 100 percent free. This includes the Asian Art Museum, the MOMA, and the Exploratorium, among many others. Although these days can be crowded, braving the hordes can be totally worth it. Make sure not to miss the opportunity to see really amazing stuff for free.

Farmer's Markets: Farmer's markets are the thing to do if you want lots of delicious and often organic produce at fair prices. Many stands at these markets offer samples, allowing you to get half-full for free. The main farmer's markets in the city can be found at: the Ferry Building Tuesday, Thursday, Saturday and Sunday until 2 p.m.; UN Plaza (between Hyde and Market Streets) Wednesday and Sunday until 5 p.m.; and 100 Alemany Blvd., until 6 p.m. There are other smaller ones throughout the City but they are not as regular. Go feed yourself and support some farmers dammit!

Rub & Tug: So you're walking through the Tenderloin when suddenly you think to yourself, "Gee, I'm really in the mood for a cheap massage topped off with an expert handjob." Well my friend, you are certainly in the right neighborhood. Unless this is your first time in a big city, you should know that all of the massage parlors you see in the Loin are more than just massage parlors. Just remember that the girls working at these spots are providing a service (mainly touching gross-ass you) and should be tipped accordingly and treated with respect. Just because they are doing what no one else wants to do to you doesn't make them subhuman.

Free Internet: This City has so much wireless Internet that you can go most places, open your laptop and be connected to the Internet for free. If this doesn't work, it's probably because you don't have a wireless card, idiot.

Leftovers: If you go out to eat and don't finish your food, get it wrapped up to go. That way even if you don't plan on eating it later, you can give it to a homeless person on your way home. They really appreciate that sort of thing.

Free Concerts: There are all kinds of opportunities to see good free music in the city. Both Amoeba Records on upper Haight and the Virgin Megastore on Market often put on live in-store concerts by nationally touring acts. Go by the stores or look online to see who is playing and when. Also, all summer long there are free concerts by the Golden Gate Park Band at the Arboretum and Botanical Gardens around 9th and Lincoln in the park. The concerts happen every Sunday and begin at 1 p.m.

Kid's Menus: If you're broke and hungry, always try to see if the restaurant will let you order off the kid's menu. The prices are always much cheaper and the portions are at least enough to stop you from being hungry.

Liquor and Delis: A corner liquor and deli can often be your best bet for a big cheap sandwich. And since the sandwiches are usually pretty big, you can always save the second half for later.

Pizza: When in doubt, there is always pizza. Pizza can be eaten for breakfast, lunch or dinner and a slice is usually cheap and filling. Also, any place where there is a high consolidation of bars, you'll find a pizza place open late.

Pay What You Can Nights: Many theaters have at least one night a month that allows you to see a show and pay only as much as you wish to give. If you're interested in seeing some shows, just drop by or call some theaters to see when they have a "pay what you can" night.

Summer Street Festivals: These are a great way to have fun, drink beer on the streets, and see free live music. Just about every weekend in the summer, a different neighborhood has a festival and the best way to find out about them is the *San Francisco Bay*

Guardian or the *San Francisco Weekly*. These publications are free and are everywhere in the City.

The Guardian/The SF Weekly: Whether you are looking for something to do or just want to read a couple good articles, grab either the *SF Bay Guardian* or the *SF Weekly* from just about any street corner in the City. Both of these publications are a good way to keep your ear to the street. From concerts to art shows to local politics, the *Guardian* and the *Weekly* are great ways to stay informed.

The Haight

For those of you who are familiar with 1960s American history, the name Haight Street should ring a bell. The intersection of Haight and Ashbury was considered the heart of hippiness in the mid-sixties, and in 1967, during the Summer of Love, it became the destination for young dropouts and wanderers from all over the nation. For a brief moment, before the influx of thousands of young street urchins, the Haight was a minor utopia with free health clinics, free concerts, a safe place to go if your acid trip went bad and even a free store (research the Diggers—www.diggers.org—they were brilliant). But we all know what happened: Flower Power failed, drugs got out of hand, the Vietnam War kept on going and more and more drifters moved in. Now the Haight is both quite different from and quite similar to what it was back in the 1960s. The area between Stanyan and Masonic, called Upper Haight, is now a very trendy shopping area filled to the gills with vintage clothing stores, smoke shops, tattoo/piercing parlors and restaurants. It also still has lots of young street kids who live in Golden Gate Park and try to sell you green buds and mushrooms, or just ask you for spare change. Lower Haight, the area from around Divisadero to Webster, is mostly bars, clubs, record stores and other weird shit including a cannabis club.

Food

...y good and cheap place to get Middle Eastern food. Nothing on the menu is more than $8 and most things are under $6. The people here are friendly and the sitting area is comfy and decorated to look, you guessed it, Middle Eastern.

All You Knead

1466 Haight St. @ Masonic Ave.

When I think of all the times I've woken up in the Haight with a hangover the size of a VW bus, All You Knead is usually the next thing that crosses my mind. This place serves giant portions of food at reasonable prices, and feels like it has been around since the days when the Grateful Dead lived within walking distance. Truthfully, the diner food here is only mediocre, but the breakfast food is perfect.

Cha Cha Cha

1801 Haight St. @ Schrader St.;
also 2327 Mission St. @ 19th St.

While it is not one of the least expensive restaurants in this book, Cha Cha Cha is one of the better and more popular ones. This restaurant sells tapas, so the best way to get the most for your money is to go with a couple people and share a few plates. The quesadillas are particularly filling, but my personal favorite is the Cajun shrimp. If you do go, try some sangria and enjoy the neat Afro-Cuban voodoo decor.

Escape From New York Pizza

1737 Haight St.;
also 333 Bush St.; 508 Castro @ 18th St.

Definitely one of my personal favorite slices, Escape from New York can be found at multiple locations around the city. Check out the Wall of Fame where people from Leonard Cohen to Jack Black have left an autograph. Make sure to try their pesto pizza; it's excellent. Most importantly though, on the first Friday of every month, the downtown location (333 Bush St. @ Montgomery St.) has a Pizza and Poetry night where you pay $5 to get all-you-can-eat pizza and hear live poetry.

Fat Slice

1535 Haight St. @ Clayton St.

Exactly as the name implies, this place has very fat slices of pizza. One week when I was really broke, I lived off two slices a day from Fat Slice. This is a great place to keep in mind if you are broke as hell and hungry as fuck.

Kate's Kitchen

471 Haight St. @ Fillmore St.

If you are willing to wait in line, Kate's Kitchen is a perfect place to work off your hangover on a Sunday. The place can be a tight squeeze on the weekends, but the prices are decent, and besides tasting great, the food comes in heaping quantities. But if you asked me what my favorite part about Kate's Kitchen is, I'd say it was the giant, insane, kinda folkloric-looking U.S. map painted on the wall.

People's Café

1479 Haight St. @ Masonic Ave.

Doesn't this totally sound like it should be in Berkeley? Well it looks like it too. There are big windows that allow you to watch all the Haight's beautiful freaks walk by while you sit and drink some fair trade coffee and eat an organic salad. The food is pretty good and so are the prices. One thing that I really like about this place is that the art is always terrific. They always have these really cool fisheye-lens photographs on display.

ᵧ ......ᵤᵣᵧₑᵣₛ and some people say they're the best things they've ever tasted.

Bars

Aub Zam Zam
1633 Haight St. @ Belvedere St.

Apparently Zam Zam was owned and operated for 50 years by a surly and eccentric man named Bruno. A few years ago, Bruno died, leaving his bar to a few friends, who to some regulars'

Aub Zam Zam looks a lot better in color. Too bad I spent that part of my budget trying to find out how many Snapple fun facts there were.

dismay, made the place a little more friendly. Truthfully, I was never around in the Bruno days, but I've always loved the look and the vibe of this place. From inside and out, this tiny bar kinda has that look of 1920s Hollywood meshed with Persia or North Africa. It's like, why isn't Humphrey Bogart sitting next to me? The jukebox is almost entirely music from the Rat Pack era or before, and the house specialty is martinis, of course. The place really is tiny—I doubt you can fit 40 people inside—but in a way, that adds to its allure. Here's lookin' at you kid.

Hobson's Choice
1601 Haight St. @ Clayton St.

Located on upper Haight, this Victorian punch house has one of the coolest happy hours around. Despite the fact that this bar has more kinds of rum than Jimmy Buffet's liquor cabinet, their specialty is a much-liquored-up punch known in frat houses around the world as Jungle Juice, but simply called House Punch here.

From 5 to 7 p.m., a glass of House Punch is only $2.50, and you can also order the most amazing nachos this side of Tijuana for around $7 to $8 (depending on what you get on them). They are piled high with mango salsa, grilled chicken, a couple kinds of

_____ ......ignt it was a vvorld
Cup year, so there were always all kinds of people hanging out at the Irish pubs at weird hours of the day. I remember being at Martin Mack's the night that Ireland played England (I think), and though I don't recall who won, I do remember that the bar was fucking mayhem. Since then, I've always liked the place. Like any Irish pub, the food is good but way overpriced. I just go to Martin Mack's for the Guinness and to watch the occasional "football" game.

Molotov's
582 Haight St. @ Steiner St.

This is definitely a dive bar, no doubt about it. Molotov's serves stiff, inexpensive drinks, has one pool table and a pinball machine. Sure the bathroom is a little stinky, and the bartenders can be surly, but Molotov's is a great place for a low profile weeknight or a loud, shit-talking weekend night.

Murio's Trophy Room
1811 Haight St. @ Shrader St.

What I gather after looking at all the trophies and pictures in this joint is that John Murio was a pseudo-famous, possibly Hawaiian tennis player in the 40's or 50's. Other than that, I don't know much about him. I do know for a fact though that well drinks in this classic Haight dive are only $3.50 and cans of Hamm's are just $2. The bartenders look meaner than they actually are, and the ceiling is covered in clever caricatures of the bar's regular patrons, drawn by Ant. This is actually one of the first bars I drank at when I moved to the City, and every time I go in there I see the same couple of old guys running game on the pool table. I mean these cats are really good at billiards.

The Noc-Noc
557 Haight St. @ Steiner St.

This is another really cool ass, low profile bar in the Lower Haight. The interior looks kinda like what Timothy Leary's place would have been like if he had lived in a cave. The DJ booth is hidden in the wall, and there are cushions so that you can sit on the ground. They don't serve hard alcohol unfortunately, but they do serve really good beer, including Red Stripe. This is one of the bars that makes drinking in the Lower Haight so enjoyable.

Toronado
547 Haight St. @ Steiner St.

Toronado is a beer lover's paradise. Just walk inside, look at the board and pick out a great beer, because that's what this place does—it serves great beer. That's kinda its thing. To get the full experience, buy a sausage next door at the Rosamunde Sausage Grill and come here and wash it down with any of the three billion beers the bar serves. Just don't go expecting lovely and serene ambience; it's not a fucking wine bar.

Trax
1437 Haight St. @ Masonic Ave.

Trax is a pseudo-trashy gay dive on upper Haight Street with a friendly vibe and great drink specials. On Tuesday night all beer is $2.50; all day Thursday well Cosmos are $2.75; on Saturday nights well cocktails are $1 from 9 to 10 p.m., $2 from 10 to 11 p.m., and $3 from 11 to midnight. The drinks are pretty damn strong too. And if you feel like getting drunk in the middle of the day, all well drinks and domestic beers are $2.50 until 7 p.m. on weekdays. These are definitely some of the best deals in town.

This is easily the most normal looking part of this bar.

Shopping

American Apparel
1615 Haight St. @ Belvedere St.

Considering that this clothing company has opened something like a million retail stores internationally in the past year, it would be kind of ridiculous if you haven't heard of them. But if you fall into this category, let me break it down real quick: American Apparel is high-quality clothing made sweatshop-free in downtown L.A. that is decently affordable and does not use any form of logo branding. A t-shirt costs between $15 to $20, but you are paying for a good product that was made responsibly, and not by exploitative labor. What's also interesting is that the founder of American Apparel, Dov Charney, is a self-described pervert who has masturbated in front of female journalists on multiple occasions. Seriously.

Anubis Warpus
1525 Haight St. @ Ashbury St.

If your list of things to do today is get a tattoo, buy a copy of *Penthouse* from 1977, find a vintage belt buckle, and peruse some local zines, then Anubis Warpus is your one-stop shop. I especially like this place because it carries the oddest selection of periodicals I've ever seen. I don't always like the Haight, but I do always like Anubis Warpus.

Amoeba Records
1855 Haight St. @ Stanyan St.

I'll make this quick. If God had a basement, it would look like Amoeba Records. What used to be a bowling alley is now arguably the best music store in the City. I'm often afraid to enter it because I worry that I'll go ape-shit, spend all my money, max out my credit card, and end up doing back alley "favors" just to pay my rent. Fuck you Amoeba Records, you magnificent bastard!

signings and readings by well-known authors. Make sure to stop in and do your part to support a small, independent business.

Bound Together
1369 Haight St. & Masonic Ave.

Bound Together is an "anarchist" book collective, and it's certainly one of the coolest places in all of San Francisco. Now I know that for a lot of people, the word anarchist has negative and ominous connotations, but that is because those people are stupid. Everyone at Bound Together works for free and the store is pretty much a non-profit. They have taken it upon themselves to disseminate progressive literature to all those who are interested in learning about what is often not mentioned through most mainstream media. You can find some truly brilliant and subversive writing in this store, and I highly recommend you at least drop in and check it out for yourself.

Piedmont Boutique
1452 Haight St. @ Masonic Ave.

When walking down the street, it's hard to miss a place that has a giant pair of legs, in stockings and heels, protruding from the top half the building. Once you see it, it's even harder to resist going in, and once you do, your eyes are treated to something quite special. Imagine if RuPaul, Dame Edna and Eddie Izzard decided to open up a store together and sell custom-made clothes. Pied-mont Boutique is a lot like that, but brighter. Things range here from expensive pink, fake snakeskin bellbottoms and handmade boas to a whole wall of earrings that go for between $2 and $6. If you plan on going to Burning Man, dressing up for Halloween or becoming a drag queen, I highly recommend stopping in here to pick up your supplies. Also stop in if you wanna get a cheap pair of earrings.

Rooky Ricardo's Records
448 Haight St. @ Fillmore St.

I remember when I first found this place. I called up all my good friends (we're all music junkies) and said, "I just found the best record store in the world." The black music that came out of places like Detroit, Memphis, Philadelphia, Chicago and Mussel Shoals from the early 60's through the mid-70's is quite possibly the best thing man has ever done. Can you think of anything more universally appealing than songs like, "My Girl", "La La Means I Love You" or "Sittin' on the Dock of the Bay"? I can't. Rooky Records has all kinds of music, but specializes in soul music and 45's. If you're into music, you should do yourself a favor and visit this wonderful store.

Sights & Entertainment

...anymore. Despite this, hippies come from all over the known world to get a peek at it and on any given night at around 4:20 a.m., you can find one puffing a bowl outside of the house. Could you imagine if you lived there and had to explain to all your guests why there is constantly a group of stoners sitting in front of your house?

Buena Vista Park
Haight St. @ Buena Vista St.

This park is quite deceptive. At first it just looks like a tiny hill of grass backed up by a short line of trees. So you think to yourself, "I'm just gonna walk to the top of the grass," but then you get to the trees and realize that they keep going. Your curiosity gets the better of you, so you decide to see how far up the trees go. It can't be that far right? It looks like such a small hill. Five minutes later you're still walking uphill and thinking, "Goddamnit. Where the hell am I going?" But by this point you figure that you might as well finish what you've started. Another five minutes later you get to the top, turn around and see half of San Francisco. You think to yourself, "My goodness, what a lovely city! I'm sure glad that I decided to walk to the top of the grass."

Club Deluxe
1511 Haight St. @ Ashbury St.

The swanky vibe of this place probably comes from its 1949 art deco design. But despite the upmarket vibe, there is almost never a cover charge here. You can catch live jazz most nights of the week except for Monday, which is stand-up comedy night, and Tuesday, which has poetry and jazz. To top everything off, the bartenders are really good at their jobs, and the bar serves gourmet pizza.

The Red Vic

1727 Haight St. between Cole & Schrader Sts.
www.redvicmoviehouse.com

This is hands down one of the best movie houses I've ever been to. They sell their own organic goodies, and instead of stadium seating they have comfortable couches. The Red Vic specializes in playing mostly (but not exclusively) independent films long after they have been initially released. Since they only have one screen, they only play a film for a couple nights. Make sure you keep up with their schedule either by stopping by to pick one up or visiting them online. They usually have their schedule picked out two months in advance.

Photo by *Trisha Gum*

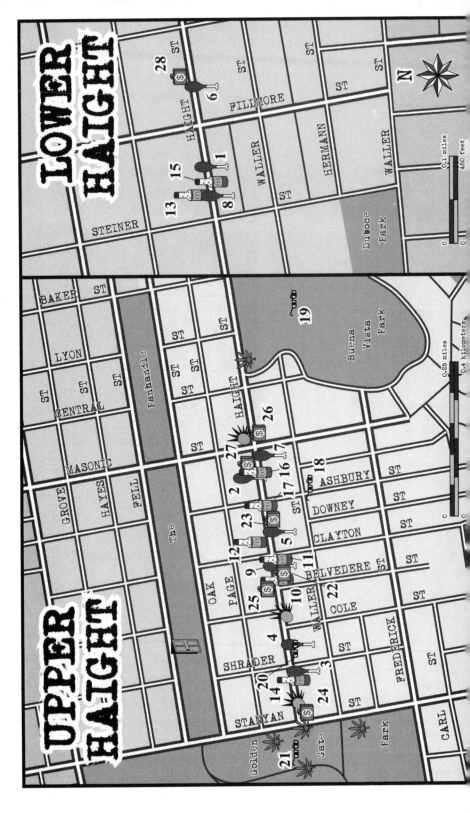

THE HAIGHT

GRUB-A-DUB-DUB

1 Ali Baba's Cafe
2 All You Knead
3 Cha Cha Cha
4 Escape From New York Pizza
5 Fat Slice
6 Kate's Kitchen
7 People's Cafe
8 Rosamunde Sausage Grill
9 Askew Grill

DRINKS DRINKS DRINKS

10 Aub Zam Zam
11 Hobson's Choice
12 Martin Mack's
13 Molotov's
14 Murio's Trophy Room
15 The Noc-Noc
16 Trax
17 Club Deluxe

PLACES TO CHE

18 710 Ashbur
    House)
19 Buena Vist
20 The Red Vic
21 Hippie Hill

SHOPPING

22 American A
23 Anubis Wart
24 Amoeba Reco
25 The Booksmi
26 Bound Toget
27 Piedmont Bo
28 Rooky Ricar

Gutter Punks a

Someone selling   rooms"

Portal to magic   a (only
visible if on sl

North Beach/ Fisherman's Wharf

North Beach is best known for three things: Italian food, strip clubs and the Beats. Because of its long history as a primarily Italian area, there are many great Italian restaurants all over the neighborhood. Unfortunately, most of them are far too pricey to make it into this book. That being said, there are still plenty of great ways to experience the Italian culture here like bakeries and delis. The Beats, on the other hand, are something far more accessible. First and foremost, you can go to City Lights Books and see where all the Beats sold their books and did poetry readings. Also, North Beach still has a thriving café scene where you can hang out, sip lattes, read a book, have moderately interesting conversations and watch really attractive people walk by. If you wanna see some naked girls, North Beach is the place for you as well. Broadway is lined with strip clubs, many of which have different deals nightly. North Beach is also cool because something about it—whether it's the layout of the narrow streets or the sound of accents—makes it feel oddly European.

Unfortunately, due to the amount of striped-shirt-wearing bridge-and-tunnel types who invade it every weekend in large numbers, North Beach does not feel as bohemian as it might have at one time. But if you look hard enough and in the right places, or just read further in this book, you can find some great little gems hidden among the pasta, poetry and panties.

Food

things that I find holy in this world—pizza and Mexican food. No, I don't mean that you can get a pizza burrito, because that would just be gross. (Or would it? Hmm.) What makes this place wondrous is that it sells both cuisines and is open until 3 a.m. Although there is absolutely nothing resembling ambience, this spot is cheap and basically perfect.

Café Trieste
609 Vallejo St. @ Grant St.

A staple of North Beach, Café Trieste has been around since the 1950s. Its strong coffee and intriguing clientele have always made Trieste a great place to sit and hang out for a couple hours. The coffee is imported and roasted on the premises (I think) and on any given day there is a good chance you'll see an impromptu acoustic jam session right outside the front door. This place really gives you a feeling of what North Beach must have been like for the Beat poets who hung out at Café Trieste 50 years ago. It also happens to be where Francis Ford Coppola wrote a lot of the *Godfather* screenplay.

El Zorro
308 Columbus Ave. @ Broadway

Although not one of the City's cheapest Mexican food joints, El Zorro is one of the less expensive places to eat in North Beach. Here you can get all your Mexican favorites like burritos, tacos and quesadillas. It's also open pretty late, so you can stop by after the bars.

Giordano Bros.

303 Columbus Ave. @ Broadway

If you're looking for a taste of Pittsburgh in the middle of North Beach then this is for you. Giordano Bros. makes what it calls the All-in-One sandwich, a sandwich that has meat, cheese, fries and coleslaw, all between two slices of bread. All of these big-ass sandwiches are $7.25 or less, and if you really want to, you can add a fried egg for $0.50. They also have TVs for sports and a giant, inflatable Pittsburgh Steelers doll. Up until this place opened, I had completely forgotten that Pittsburgh existed.

Golden Boy Pizza

542 Green St. @ Grant St.

Sicilian-style pizza at its best, Golden Boy is a staple of North Beach. Go there for a slice and/or a beer, but make sure you get there before last call because the line gets long once the nearby bars close.

In-N-Out Burger

333 Jefferson St. @ Jones St.

If you couldn't tell by now, I'm not much for big corporations or fast food. First of all, they don't need my business, or any hype from me; and secondly, most of them are shady, insidious businesses that care far more about money than they do about people. That being said, I wouldn't be doing justice to the title of Broke-Ass if I excluded In-N-Out Burger from this guide. The burgers here are so delicious that a friend of mine walked all the way from Upper Haight to *Daly fucking City* to get one—I shit you not. The food is tremendously cheap, the workers are paid considerably competitive wages, and you can get a hamburger as big as your imagination. Try the 4x4: four beef patties and four slices of cheese. Damn, I should be on the payroll of the Cardiologist's Union of America for that last sentence.

Juicy Lucy's

703 Columbus Ave. @ Filbert St.

To be honest, raw and organic food places aren't always the

Mario's Bohemian Cigar Store

566 Columbus Ave. @ Union St.

All I have to say is: *grilled foccacia sandwiches bitches*! The sandwiches at Mario's are so good that you have to stop yourself from making moans of pleasure while you eat. Mario's is a good place to grab a bite and have a beer or glass of wine. The staff is friendly and sociable, the music is pretty good, and did I mention that they have amazing grilled foccacia sandwiches? Well they do.

Naan 'n Curry

533 Jackson St. @ Columbus

(see entry on page 208)

Palermo Deli

1556 Stockton St. @ Union St.

This excellent Italian deli is run by a Joe Peschi-ish guy named Frankie and his brother Vince. These are some really good guys, who deserve every good thing that comes to them, and who also make delicious fucking sandwiches. Straight up. One of my favorite things to do is stop by Palermo, get a sandwich on some nicely toasted ciabatta bread and go sit in Washington Square Park to read a book and look at girls sunbathing. That, my friends, is truly a little slice of heaven.

Sam's Pizza and Burgers

618 Broadway @ Grant St.

To be quite honest, North Beach can be a pretty shitty place some-times. On the weekends you get a lot of people who just wanna spend tons of money, look flashy, pick fights and in general, be assholes. That's their thing, whatever. But according to some of my older friends (as well as books and movies), North Beach ac-tually used to be a really cool place where neat and artistic things took place (like when my friend had Charles Bukowski come and read at her house in the late 70's). Like Vesuvio and Spec's, Sam's is a glimpse into what North Beach must have been like before ... well before now. Don't get me wrong, there is absolutely *noth-ing* neat or artistic about Sam's, it's just a greasy spoon diner for fuck's sake, but it's a real diner for real people who don't want to spend $10 on a beer just to be around other people willing to spend $10 on a beer. Sam's is only open from 5 p.m. to 2 a.m., but I bet you'll meet more interesting people in one drunken food excursion here than you will in two months of partying at places like Impala or Dolce.

Sushi Hunter

1701 Powell St. @ Union St.

Going to Sushi Hunter is like having a party in your belly where the only ones invited are copious amounts of sushi and sake. And I mean copious. For $22.95 you get all the sushi you can eat. Granted you have to choose off the designated all-you-can-eat menu, but it has more than 50 items. And if that wasn't enough, for an extra $12 you get all the sake you can drink. Holy shit, right? It reminds me of back in high school when my buddies and I would get really high and then descend on Hometown Buffet like a Mongol Horde attacking an Eastern European village. I think we'd even take turns going out to the parking lot for bong-load breaks so we could keep eating. But I digress ... back to the matter at hand: for $34.95 you can get all the sushi and sake your little hearts desire!

B○──

hour on, and this is specifically because they have a buy-one-drink-get-one-free deal. Their happy hour goes till 9 p.m., which means you can be completely shit-faced by the time everyone else is just leaving their houses.

Gino & Carlo
548 Green St. @ Grant St.

Gino & Carlo is the type of place your cool Italian grandfather would hang out at, sitting around and bullshitting about Rocky Marciano and Joe Frazier. The patron saints of this bar are the Rat Pack, and photos of sports heroes like DiMaggio and Joe Montana line the walls. Walking in, you feel like everyone is a regular but you. It's not a menacing feeling; it's just that they've probably all been drinking here since before the first Super Bowl. This is a great place to wind down your night, and an even better place to spend your Sunday afternoon. During football season, they lay out a table full of free food. Just don't act a fool in this place because you might get ... uh, taken care of.

Kennedy's
1040 Columbus Ave. @ Jones St.

This is the only Irish pub I've ever been to that has an Indian curry house in the center of it. Kennedy's has plenty of pool tables and video games as well as perfectly surly bartenders, but the best part about this odd little place is that pitchers of Pabst Blue Ribbon are only $7. During happy hour (5 to 7 p.m.), PBR pitchers are only $5, pints of Guinness are $2 and if you buy any pint, you get a free drink token redeemable anytime. So go to Kennedy's and buy a friend a drink, or hell, a pitcher.

Mr. Bing's
201 Columbus Ave. @ Pacific St.

Mr. Bing's is a good solid place to drink. The large V-shaped bar, in this small boxy space, takes up most of the room, and there are a dozen billiards trophies on display despite the bar not having a pool table. The shape of the bar makes meeting other derelicts

Even Freud would be perplexed by my weird neon light fetish.

quite easy because they are only 15 feet away and you're looking right at them. The drinks here are stupidly strong and the beef jerky sold behind the counter always hits the spot. I've been there on nights where almost every time someone took a shot, so did the bartender. It's that type of joint.

Saloon
1232 Grant St. @ Columbus Ave.

From the outside, this spot has a total biker bar look to it, but once you get in you realize that it is more of a 55-year-olds-getting-drunk-and-dancing sort of spot. This fabled watering hole is one of the oldest in the City, and didn't burn down during the fire/earthquake of 1906 because the firemen wanted to save what was at the time also one of the City's favorite whorehouses. Though the whores are gone, the bar is still here serving $3 well drinks and offering live music (mostly blues) every night. Make sure to check out the stained glass windows near the front. Last night the bartender carded my friends and after they explained that they were carded at the door, the barkeep answered, "By who? That guy doesn't work here." So what if the crowd is old, smells a little, and is usually shit-faced drunk? The Saloon might just be the bar that all other dives are trying to emulate.

a bar of some sort has almost always inhabited the site since the building was constructed in the 1800s. Plus Jack Dempsey worked here before becoming heavyweight champion of the world.

Specs Twelve Adler Museum Café (Specs)
12 Adler St. (Right next to 250 Columbus) @ Broadway
As evidenced by the news clippings next to the entrance, much has been written about Specs. From what I gather, Specs Simmons (named for his spectacles) bought the bar with the money he made from the 60's folk single "Ridin' the MTA" and decorated the bar with things he gathered during his travels as a merchant marine. How much of this is true, I don't know. There are as many rumors about Specs as there are articles written about it. Simply put, Specs feels like a Tom Waits song. There's crazy shit all over the walls, like photos of post fire/earthquake S.F., 500-year-old Hindu art, and an actual dead cobra and groundhog posed to look like they are fighting each other. The drinks are strong, the well vodka is bad … what else could you possibly want from a dive bar?

Sweetie's
475 Francisco St. @ Mason St.
Sweetie's is a lovely little local bar where well drinks are $3.50, the bar staff is friendly and there's an art gallery in the back. They also have good artwork lining the walls throughout the bar.

My favorite of all the little touches (and there are many) is the medieval looking chandelier that hangs over the pool table. The only bad thing about this bar is that it closes early—10:30 p.m. on weekdays and 11 p.m. on weekends.

Tosca
242 Columbus Ave. @ Kearny St.

This is a really neat bar. I always feel like it's the 1940s when I'm inside. The actual bar where people sit is the longest I've ever seen. It's got these big metal steam machines for espresso drinks on each end and usually has one of the Rat Pack playing on the jukebox. The bartenders all wear tuxedo shirts and bow ties and usually offer something interesting to your conversation. Tosca is not the cheapest bar in North Beach, but it is definitely one of the coolest. Their specialty is a drink whose name I don't remember; but it involves hot chocolate and liquor and is exquisite.

Vesuvio
255 Columbus Ave. @ Broadway

Vesuvio is a cool little bar in North Beach famous because the Beats used to hang out there. Because of its close proximity to City Lights, Vesuvio's literary clientele can often be seen reading, or talking about reading, while enjoying a drink. In fact, Vesuvio is probably the only bar in the city where James Joyce comes up more often than the 49ers. It's a great place to have a few drinks and meet some interesting people. And if you get there early enough, you can get a window seat upstairs and watch all of North Beach pass by. Also, Vesuvio opens up at 6 a.m. for you real alcoholics.

Vesuvio is one of the best bars in the world. Seriously.

Shopping

101 Basement
513 Green St. @ Grant St.

I love music. I've probably got around 1,000 albums between the CDs, records and tapes, and for anyone who loves music (and getting good deals on music), 101 Basement is fundamentally the biggest set of blueballs you could ever imagine. Basically, the upstairs is filled with instruments, most of them common and a few antique and unusual, but the downstairs is a humongous basement filled with probably more than 100,000 records. The rub is that there is little to no organization to the way the records are displayed. So you could spend days on end searching through crap before you find anything good. If you're a serious collector or have lots of time on your hands, I wish you the best of luck. Your best bet is to do a little speed before heading down there.

City Lights Books
261 Columbus Ave. @ Broadway

I don't even know where to begin talking about City Lights. This bookseller/publishing house has been independently owned by poet Lawrence Ferlinghetti for more than 50 years. Back in the days when all the Beat writers were hanging around North Beach, City Lights was a place where their books could be sold and they could read their poetry. There are even pictures from the early 60's of Bob Dylan hanging out there. City Lights was the first all paperback book store in the U.S., and its publishing house has put out much of Allen Ginsberg's work (including *Howl* and *Kaddish*) as well as books by Charles Bukowski. Go to City Lights and read a book; it'll be good for you.

International Spy Shop

555 Beach St. @ Leavenworth St.

I doubt that there is actually anything cheap here, but ~~~~ ~~

Z.Cioccolato

474 Columbus Ave. @ Green St.

CANDY!!!! If you feel like giving a subtle fuck you to your dentist, drop in and check out Z.Cioccolato. Here you can buy candy in bulk as well as truffles and homemade fudge. But the best thing of all is that they let you sample almost anything you want, as long as you're not a greedy little piggy who takes too much.

Sights & Entertainment

The Beat Museum
540 Broadway @ Columbus Ave.

I really like a lot of the Beat stuff, so this place was a real treat for me. They have all sorts of original pressings of various Beat classics like *On the Road*, a whole exhibit about the obscenity trial for Allen Ginsburg's *Howl*, and a weird section about whether this one guy found a piece of Sputnik in his backyard. If you read Jack Kerouac when you were 17 and he made you want to hitchhike around the country, this museum is for you. If I remember right, it costs about $5 to get in.

Bimbo's 365
1025 Columbus Ave. @ Chestnut St.
www.bimbo365club.com

Although it first opened on Market Street in 1931, Bimbo's, in all its opulence and elegance, has been sitting at its current location since 1951. Needless to say, it's been around for a minute. Rita Hayworth used to be a Can-Can girl here. In recent years acts like Lenny Kravitz, Macy Gray, Blonde Redhead and Seu Jorge have played. It's really a crapshoot—some shows are pretty damn expensive and some are affordable, but half of what you're paying for is ambience. It really feels like this was the most glamorous place in SF in the 50's and that nothing has changed. I think they even still have a girl swimming in the fish tank sometimes. Now that's class.

Broadway Tunnel
Tunnel on Broadway that connects North Beach to Polk St.

Most people probably don't think that there is anything particularly impressive about this tunnel other than the astounding amount of soot that has built up on its walls over the years. But since I'm not most people, I think the tunnel is absolutely wonderful. What I love about it is that when you walk through it, and the cars

ture is almost impossible to miss if you are in North Beach. Getting to the tower requires quite a bit of uphill walking (or just a little bit of uphill driving if you have a car), but once you get there you will be blessed with one of the best views in all of San Francisco. You can go inside the tower for free to check out the depression era murals sponsored by FDR's public works project, but it costs money if you want to get to the top of the tower. Telegraph Hill is also full of other neat stuff. There are architecturally astounding houses, wonderfully unique garden-like paths, and the Filbert steps, a set of stairs that lead to a street that can only be reached by the steps. Also, if you hear a bunch of birds chattering and it doesn't sound like pigeons or seagulls, it's because Telegraph Hill is home to a flock of wild parrots.

Crissy Field

What was once a military airfield has been turned into a lovely public park. On any given weekend you can see people jogging, new parents pushing strollers, dog owners walking their pets and weekend dads playing Frisbee with their kids. On a warm day it's a gorgeous place to hang out with a bottle of wine and some food and watch the boats sail around the bay with the Marin Headlands and the Golden Gate Bridge as their backdrop. Not bad, huh?

Musée Mechanique
Pier 45

www.museemechanique.org

It's really quite hard to describe this place without sounding like an eighth grader, but it really is *so fucking cool!!!* Basically, it's like a museum of arcade games with everything from modern shit like Indiana Jones pinball machines to antique penny nudie peepshows to fortuneteller machines (like in the movie *Big*). It's totally free to get in and check out all the weird things that are beeping, ringing and dinging, but to really experience it, I recommend bringing a bag of coins. That way you get to take part in the madness.

Washington Square Park
Columbus Ave. @ Union St.

About as different from the park with the same name in NYC as possible (meaning no old guys playing chess and no Jamaicans selling fake weed), this park is a small square of grass with some trees, a little playground and a statue of Ben Franklin, not George Washington. Go figure. Although there are few better places to hang out in San Francisco on a warm sunny day, my favorite time to be here is around 9:30 a.m. when all the old Chinese are doing their daily tai chi and aerobics. This one old lady brings out a sword and does her tai chi with it. How gangster is she?

PIER 39

43
41
43 1/2

NORTH
BEACH

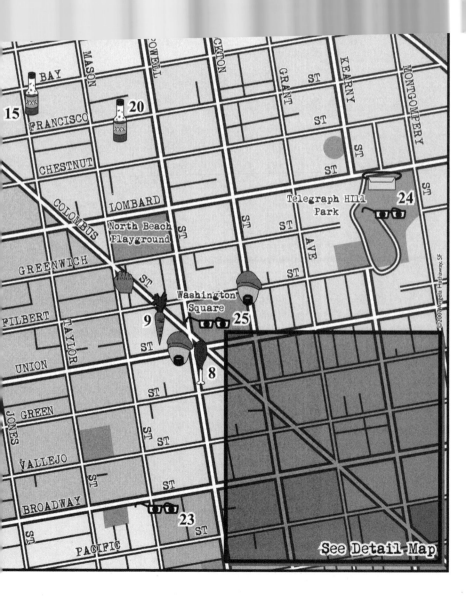

BAY
15
FRANCISCO
MASON
POWELL
STOCKTON
GRANT ST
KEARNY ST
MONTGOMERY

20

CHESTNUT

COLUMBUS
LOMBARD
North Beach
Playground
Telegraph Hill
Park
24

GREENWICH
AVE

FILBERT
TAYLOR
Washington
Square
9
25

UNION

8

JONES
GREEN

VALLEJO

BROADWAY
23

PACIFIC

See Detail Map

©2007 Angela Hathaway, SF

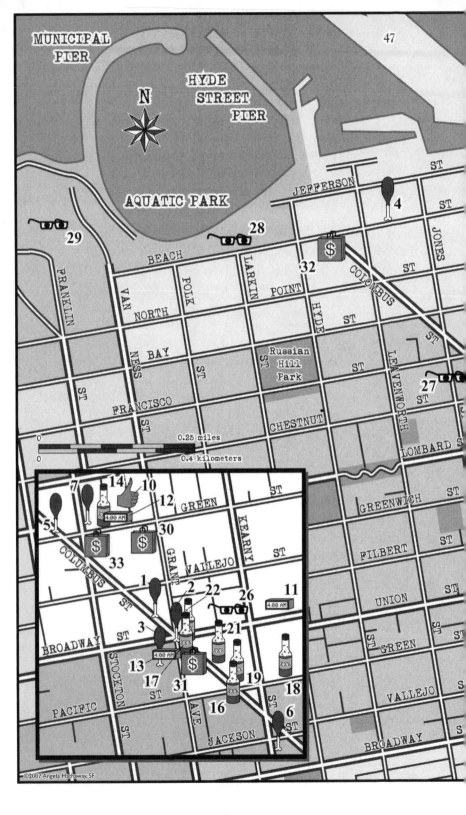

NORTH BEACH

 Wandering old beatniks

Tourists

Dudes who come from San Jose or the East Bay who go to strip shows and then walk around in groups of ten all agitated, starting fights because they're not getting laid.

The Broke-Ass Stuart Eye Spy Game

Here's how you play. Below are descriptions of some of the most notable and noticeable people in San Francisco. Some of them are local political figures, others are cultural icons, while others are just local nutcases. Which one is which is up for interpretation. See if you can spot them all.

Tobias Womack

Frank Chu (12 Galaxies guy): It's impossible to miss Frank Chu. From anti-war rallies to Bay to Breakers you can find him anywhere there's a large crowd. He's the guy carrying the sign that reads "12 Galaxies" followed by an ever-changing bunch of other words. I think he's coolest when he's wearing his dark sunglasses, which is always.

The Bushman: The Bushman has to be the richest street performer ever! For the past 25 years or so he's been taking a little bit of shrubbery, hiding behind it, then jumping out and growling at passersbys at Fisherman's Wharf. People practically shit their pants, and then give him money like, "Ha ha, you got me that time, you clever fellow, you."

Vivian and Marian Brown: These semi-famous elderly twins have been seen in all sorts of commercials from Reebok to Macy's. They dress identically and walk in step with each other every-

Powell St. Tap Dancer: This guy is absolutely incredible. I've never seen anyone tap dance like him. The best part about it is that he makes tap dancing relevant by incorporating modern music. You can find him sweating his ass off at the Cable Car turn around at the intersection of Powell and Market. Give the man a dollar, because he's really working hard.

No Sex Before Marriage Guy: This guy is so ridiculous that he's entertaining; I wonder if maybe it's just a big piece of performance art because *no one* takes him seriously. Every day he sits right by the crosswalk at Powell and Market with a sign that reads, "No Sex Before Marriage" in large, bold letters. He says things to couples like, "No sloppy seconds," and one time, when a lesbian couple passed him holding hands, I heard him mutter, "Sinners." The best days are when he brings the bullhorn.

Valencia Guitar Guy: If you've ever walked down Valencia from 16th Street to 24th Street, chances are you've seen this guy. He's kinda got the whole burnt-out-hippie thing going on, wearing weird clothes and playing guitar, but the cool thing about this guy is that he is constantly rocking the fuck out. It doesn't matter that he has no audience; he gyrates and jumps around like he's on stage in front of thousands of people. I can never understand what he's singing about though.

Mission St. Bloody Foot Guy: I often see this guy sitting outside the Walgreen's at 23rd and Mission, but I've seen him other places as well. Every time I see him he's got this gigantic gash on his foot that's just oozing blood everywhere. What baffles me is that I've seen him for probably the past three years and *every* time he's got the same thing going on. Really, how long can you bleed for? The one time I offered to get him some medical supplies he said "No," and then went into some crazy-ass story about SF General Hospital and walking to the radio towers. But my favorite was the time he asked my friends and me for change and after we said no, he called after us, "Come on guys, just buy me a taco … I get you some pussy!" We all shuddered in unison.

Robot Girl: Robot Girl goes to Union Square dressed as a robot, puts on some music and then dances a robot dance. I think she makes pretty good money doing her thing. What I like about her is that, even when she rides the bus, she rocks the robot gear and says nothing.

Michael Swaine (The Sewing Guy): On the fifteenth of every month, from noon to 6 p.m., head down to the Tenderloin and look for Michael Swaine. He'll be the guy pushing along the cart with the sewing machine on it. Swaine offers his services for free once a month, so don't miss an opportunity to get your favorite jacket sewn up.

Flower Guy: I usually see this guy walking around North Beach, the TenderNob and Union Square. It's impossible to miss him because, if you're a woman, or just walking next to a woman, he'll come up and try to offer you a flower. He's got the whole scraggly-homeless-Jesus look going on. I wonder if his whole flower bit has ever actually gotten him laid.

Willie Brown: Willie Brown is the former Mayor of San Francisco and is also one of the slickest and best-dressed motherfuckers I've ever seen in my life. He's always got on a fine-ass suit and matching fedora. It's gotta be stressful to look that sharp all the time.

...gossip.). That being said, he's still fairly popular, and awfully good looking, so I'd be willing to bet he gets reelected. I guess we'll just have to wait and see.

Smiley: Easily the best-dressed street performer I've ever seen, Smiley hangs out in front of Saks at Union Square, singing tunes and making people smile. He's probably got hundreds of different colored suits at home. I wish I had this guy's wardrobe.

Dr. Jang: If you watch TV for a while in SF, you're bound to come across Dr. Jang. He's got these commercials for his dentistry practice that are so cheesy they're almost delicious. Every time someone in the commercial finishes what they're saying, they flash the biggest, fakest smile in the world; then Jang, the main man himself, comes on at the end and totally outdoes everyone else's smile. It's like he's not even pretending the smile is real, it's so goddamn big. I think if I ever saw someone do that in real life, I'd throw up out of sheer confusion.

Castro Overalls Guy: Ever since I started working in the Castro about a year ago, I've seen this guy roughly every three days or so, and every time I see him he's wearing exactly the same thing—cutoff denim overalls, with no shirt, every single day. It's like he either has only one pair and wears them day in and day out, or he's got a closet full of just cutoffs. I can imagine him opening up his closet and saying to himself, "Hmm ... what to wear today?" I know he's got a longish beard, and I think he wears a sun hat and work boots, but I'm really not sure. I'm always too focused on his overalls to pay much attention to anything else.

Poster Pirate: Ever wonder who tapes up all those posters along Haight Street that advertise upcoming concerts? From what I gather, it's all one guy. He also hits up the 11th Street and Folsom area. One of my old roommates used to call him the Poster Pirate because she said that if you put up a poster and he comes along, he'll take down yours and replace it with one of his. Whether this is true, I don't know, but what I do know is that watching him do his poster thing is pretty crazy. He's got this whole system that allows him to take off posters and then put more up at a very fast pace. Next time you're on Haight, look around for him. He's a little inconspicuous, so you might miss him altogether.

Emperor Norton: You can't actually see this one because he's been dead for the past 120 years, but he's so uniquely and genuinely San Francisco, and kinda the great grandfather of everyone else on this list, so I figured I'd put him in. In 1859, Joshua Norton declared himself to be the "Emperor of the United States and the Protector of Mexico". Even though no one took him or his declarations seriously (his ideas included dissolving the Union and abolishing Congress), the citizens of San Francisco humored him and were glad to consider him one of their own. Norton was the first one to suggest building a bridge and tunnel from SF to Oakland, and he was probably the first local to admit that he hated it when people called the City "Frisco." He was so loved in SF that the Board of Supervisors allocated money to pay for his elaborate uniform and businesses accepted the bank notes that he made as real currency. One rumor has it that Mark Twain based the character of the King in *The Adventure of Huckleberry Finn* on Emperor Norton. Anyway, I'm not gonna sit here and write a book report, but you should definitely Google Emperor Norton and read up on him. He is about as truly San Francisco as a person can get.

The Sisters of Perpetual Indulgence: If you've ever walked through San Francisco and seen someone who looked like a cross between a drag queen, a geisha, a nun and a clown, then you've

Union Square/ Financial District

Ever since the first street plans were made for San Francisco, Union Square has been a public space. The four streets that make up this space's borders are Geary, Stockton, Powell and Post. Though it has been through many incarnations, today Union Square is an open plaza with benches, shrubbery, a little stage, an expensive café and a centered statue that was erected after Admiral Dewey's 1903 victory in the Spanish-American War. When talking about Union Square though, there is more to take into consideration than just the plaza—the name has come to define one of the main commercial centers for the whole Bay Area. Stores like Louis Vuitton and Armani line the streets surrounding the plaza, while expensive restaurants and upscale lounges dot the area just beyond. One of my favorite pastimes is to sit in Union Square reading and watching beautiful people go by. But truthfully, when it comes to shopping, I can't afford shit around here.

The Financial District is just east of Union Square and is exactly what the name implies: men in ties and women in business suits doing jobs in cubicles and making all kinds of money. This area has some very nice places to eat and drink, but most of them have absolutely no reason to be in this book. But if you just read a little further you'll be pleasantly surprised at some of the special little deals that your dear friend Broke-Ass Stuart has found for you. Since this area is so expensive, the deals are that much sweeter.

Food

joint. You can get a three-item plate with rice or chow mein for $6.99.

Bangkok Best
301 Kearny St. @ Bush St.

Like many of the eateries in this little stretch of the City, Bangkok Best receives a heavy amount of lunchtime business from all the financial district worker bees who earn their massive incomes in nearby offices. Having the foresight to capitalize on this, the good people at Bangkok Best have put together a superb lunch menu in which you get an entrée, fried wonton, Thai salad, rice and soup for as little as $7.95. The Gang Panang (#6 on the menu) is the bomb, baby!

Blondie's Pizza
63 Powell St. @ Ellis St.

The S.F. location, situated perfectly next to Rasputin Music in downtown, is a great way to feed yourself if you need a quick bite. More than just being a pizza joint, you can also get fried goodies like chicken fingers and onion rings. Besides being good to your belly, Blondie's is also good to the environment by making most all of their stuff recyclable or compostable.

China Fun Express
211 Kearny St. @ Sutter St.

In general, I'm always a little bit skeptical of any restaurant with the word "fun" in its name. What's so fun about a Chinese food buffet that sells food for $4.98 a pound? Sure it's inexpensive, but fun? Come on, Chuck E. Cheese's is fun. Chuck E. Cheese's has a six-foot-tall rat walking around giving out balloons and hugs, and slides that drop you into a ball pit that smells like feet and is probably full of lice and pink eye. That shit is fun. Chinese fast food—not quite as fun. I gotta tell you China Fun Express; you should either change your name or put some slides in your restaurant.

King of Thai Noodle

184 O'Farrell St. @ Powell St.; *also* 639 Clement St. @ 7th Ave.; 420 Geary Blvd. @ Mason St.; and tons of other locations around the City.

I am currently obsessed with Thai cuisine. The food has such a wonderful blend of flavors, and it's almost always very afford-able. King of Thai Noodle is by far the purplest Thai restaurant in all of San Francisco, and I do mean that literally. The whole place has a periwinkle theme (is that really a color?), even down to the to-go menus. The portions here are tremendous, and be-lieve it or not the people at the O'Farrell location speak English, Thai, Japanese, Spanish, Mandarin and Hebrew. It's like the United Nations, but with better food.

L&L Hawaiian Barbecue

312 Kearny St. @ Bush St.

Whatchu' know about grilled Spam sandwiches, sucka? Truth-fully I don't know much about them; the only time I ever ate Spam was once during freshman year of college when my room-mate and I got really stoned and realized that for some reason we had a can of Spam in our dorm. But Spam is apparently a staple of Hawaiian cuisine, and if you feel so inclined you can buy some, grilled, at L&L for $1.69. Everything else on the menu is pretty cheap too; most of the food costs fewer than five bucks.

Lori's Diner

501 Powell St. @ Sutter St.; also 149 Powell St. @
O'Farrell St.; and 336 Mason St. @ Geary Blvd.

food. It's not the cheapest diner in the city, but you can find almost
whatever food you're looking for here and the one on Mason is
open 24 hours. As a side note, if you're ever in San Diego, check out
the Corvette Diner, it's the best 50's diner this side of 1959.

Ramzi's Café

44 Montgomery St. @ Market St.

Ramzi's is the kind of spot in the bottom of a big office building,
where your parents would send you to get chips or something on
the days they took you to work with them. Like when you were
bugging them because you were bored, and they just wanted you
out of their hair. Simply put, Ramzi's is just an office building deli.
But it is also extremely cheap. Before 11 a.m. you can get a breakfast burrito for $2.75, and everything else is less than $6.50.

Segafredo

235 Powell St. @ O'Farrell St.

It's weird; in the Union Square area all the eateries are either nice,
expensive sit-down places, or unimpressive hurry-the-fuck-up-
and-eat-so-we-can-get-more-customers type of places. Segafredo
falls into the second category. The way it works is you walk in,
order one of the pre-made dishes that you see behind the glass,
then go to the back and eat it. The eating area is shared with the
Chinese place next door, Asia Express, and also with the pizza
place next door to that. The food's not bad, and it's a quick bite.

Tasty Express

336 Kearny St. @ Pine St.

Well, "tasty" is a relative thing I guess, but "express" isn't. This place serves up pan-Asian food (Chinese, Vietnamese, Thai, etc.) by the pound; $4.48 a pound to be exact. Sometimes in life that's about as much as you can ask for.

Tomato & Basil

305 Kearny St. @ Bush St.

I was in here the other day and it smelled *so good.* The guy behind the counter told me that the smell was emanating from him but I'm pretty sure it came from the chicken in the rotisserie oven just behind him (I'm not falling for that trick again). Either way, this joint has pretty decent food, most of which is far below the $6 mark. I also like the way their awning is painted; it's kinda whimsical ... and I'm kinda weird.

...y ...properly describe the Gold Dust is "unique." It has been open since the 1930s with the interior undoubtedly unchanged,

The Gold Dust Lounge has all the charm of a Victorian-era saloon without the threat of a cholera outbreak. What more could you ask for?

and it is probably the only Union Square bar that won't empty your wallet. The truly amazing thing about the Gold Dust is that it perfectly rides the line between absolute cheesiness and utter brilliance. The walls and ceilings look fake Victorian, and the nightly band (four of its five members are named John) can and will play anything for a tip. The bar also has a long and interesting history—just ask the bartender about the secret passageway.

The Holding Company

2 Embarcadero Center

This is the type of old school joint where there's always sports on the TV and the bartenders wear ties and tell dirty jokes. One guy talked us into having a shot called the Bird-Flu shot; it was blue and delicious. They also have free food Tuesday through Thursday during happy hour when pints are a dollar off and pitchers are four bucks off. Easily the coolest thing though is the dishwasher. It basically functions like a miniature drive through car wash, and they call it "The Cadillac" because when the place bought their first one in 1980, it cost the same as a brand new Caddy.

MacArthur Park
607 Front St. @ Jackson St.

I can't believe they let me in this place! I mean most of my clothes have holes in them. Although this is the type of place that I could never afford to eat at normally, their happy hour has free appetizers. Hooray for free food! Just buy a drink and then keep going back for as much food as you can stomach. The food is different each day of the week (I think they only do it on weekdays). Some days it's just cheese, fruit and crackers, others, it's Buffalo wings and potato skins. Don't say I never gave you nothing. Stick with me kid, and I'll show you the world.

Morton's Steakhouse
400 Post St. @ Powell St.

I am a golden god for giving this one to you! Yes my friends, this one here is fucking gorgeous! Every Monday-Friday from 5 to 7 p.m., this super high-grade, upscale steakhouse offers FREE all you can eat mini-filet-mignon sandwiches if you buy a drink at the bar. The one drawback is the cost of a drink; a bottle of Budweiser is $6.50. But come on, you know it's totally worth it. P.S. I guess the whole golden god thing doesn't apply if you're a vegetarian. Sorry, celery munchers.

Palio D'Asti
640 Sacramento St. @ Montgomery St.

I'm amazed to find how many amazing happy hour deals exist in some of the City's finer restaurants. A main course here during dinner can cost as much as $31, but Monday through Friday from 4 to 7 p.m. you get a free slice of pizza if you buy two drinks. Okay, so this obviously isn't the best happy hour in the book, but the pizza is pretty good.

Ponzu
401 Taylor St. @ O'Farrell St.

The food at this upscale Union Square rest~

~mutherfucker. That's who.

Betta recognize, suckas!

The Tonga Room
940 Mason St. @ California St.

The Tonga Room is a really fucking bizarre place. Although it is by no means the least expensive place in this book, you get quite a bit for what you pay for. To begin with, the Tonga Room is in the super bourgeois Fairmont Hotel up on Nob Hill. At some point, the hotel had an indoor pool where the Tonga Room is currently located and instead of getting rid of the pool, they decided to build a Tiki styled bar/restaurant around it. They have this floating stage that comes out every once in awhile with an all-Chinese band that plays covers of American pop songs, and every ten minutes or so it thunders and rains on the pool. Very Vegas, baby. Anyway, for their happy hour you pay something like eight bucks, and buy one drink (a beer is at least $5) and you get to eat all the appetizers you can. And this ain't just cheese and crackers; they have all sorts of very good food (I can't tell you specifically because it has been awhile since I was last there). Anyway, line your pockets with plastic, and fill them up with as much food as you can.

Shopping

Fashion SF
362 Kearny St. @ Pine St.

When your aunt comes to San Francisco with the sole mission of finding a good knock-off Burberry purse, send her to Fashion SF. Not that I know much of what I'm talking about here, but this place seems to have decent quality goods, all of which are fakes. Do you think Louis Vuitton makes body bags? If so, do you think people would buy knock-offs?

H&M
150 Powell St. @ O'Farrell St.

A big chain store that sells reasonably-priced, fashionable clothes. Should this even be in here? I guess so cuz it's cheap but ... well ... you know how you try to shop ethically, supporting independent business and not buying sweatshop-made clothing, but at the same time you're totally broke and also want to look good? I guess H&M fully encompasses that dilemma.

Rasputin Music
69 Powell St. @ Ellis St.

This is really a fine record store, and lucky for you, it's right in the middle of everything, making it easy for you to shop there. Please stop buying music (and anything else for that matter) at places like Best Buy (or even Starbucks, for fuck's sake). It cheapens all of us. Support independent music retailers like Rasputin because they actually give a shit about music. I'm very serious. If we continue to shop at giant retailers and buy all our goods online, there aren't gonna be *any* independent places left to shop at. That will make me cry, and unlike Chuck Norris, my tears don't cure cancer, they just taste like salt.

highly recommend checking him out if you're looking for jewelry.

Sights & Entertainment

Art Galleries

There are loads of art galleries in the Union Square area. Chances are you can't afford anything in them (or at least I can't), but if you've got some free time, just wander around and check some of them out. A few of the galleries carry work by really famous artists like Andy Warhol and Picasso, but my favorites are the galleries that carry stuff by artists I've never heard of. The 444 gallery (444 Post @ Powell) always has really interesting and colorful stuff created by artists in Eastern Europe and South America. Also check out 49 Geary St., which is an entire building filled with art galleries and rare bookstores. I would love to collect art; the only problem is that you gotta have a lot of money to do it.

Bonkers
483 Pine St. @ Kearny St.

Remember video arcades? Bonkers might be one of the only places in all of the City that is still completely devoted to being one. But considering half the machines don't work and there's never anyone in there, I'm convinced that it has to be a front for the Chinese mafia. Regardless, where else are you gonna go to play Street Fighter 2?

Frank Lloyd Wright Building
140 Maiden Ln. @ Stockton St.

Frank Lloyd Wright is probably the most famous and inventive American architect. His work is known for blending into its surroundings to make the structure look like it occurred naturally. Although he designed many buildings and houses in California

(Palo Alto supposedly has the most), to my knowledge the only one in San Francisco currently houses the store Xanadu. The shop

Palace Hotel
2 New Montgomery @ Market St.

While there is no fucking way I could afford to stay in a place like this, that doesn't mean that I can't go in and look at the lobby. This is one of the coolest lobbies in all of San Francisco, mainly because of the Garden Court, a Victorian-era lounge that is quite reminiscent of the Plaza Hotel in Manhattan. What's also interesting about the Palace is that it's where President Warren G. Harding died on August 23rd, 1923.

Union Square
The big square park in the middle

One of my favorite things to do on a sunny day is to go down to Union Square with a book and just hang out. If you're single and not shy, it's a great place to meet cute people from around the globe. Think about it like this: if you see some hottie reading *Lonely Planet* or some other guide book, (maybe a *Broke-Ass Stuart Guide*?) just sit by them and say, "Hi there. Where you from?" Suddenly you have something to talk about, and who knows what can happen? Same goes for someone who's not a tourist—just sit by them and say something simple like, "What a lovely day, huh?" You never know what kind of cool people you'll meet or interesting conversations you might get into. Even if you're not there to meet people, it's great for people watching and sprawling out on the grass and passing out. Homeless people do it all the time.

Wells Fargo History Museum
420 Montgomery St. @ California St.

What's cool about this free museum is that it makes you realize the history of Wells Fargo is inextricably tied to that of San Francisco. Inside they have a real stagecoach, as well as actual gold dust and nuggets. In the back corner are two telegraph machines thirty or so feet from each other that allow you to send messages between them. (Do you think telegraph sex was the precursor to phone sex?) The staff is very helpful and friendly, and the pictures on the wall all date from before the 1906 earthquake and fire.

If you are a big history dork like myself, you'll love this place. It makes the California Historical Society Museum look like a little bitch.

The last thing I remember is taking of sip of Tobias's bottle of Jameson. The next thing I know I'm on top of a freeway overpass with a typewriter. At least it's better than that time I ended up in Bakersfield. Photo by Tobias Womack

UNION SQUARE/ FINANCIAL DISTRICT

UNION SQUARE

GRUB-A-DUB-DUB

1 Asia Express
2 Bangkok Best
3 Blondie's Pizza
4 King of Thai Noodle
5 China Fun Express
6 L&L Hawaiian
  Barbeque
7 Ramzi's Cafe
8 Segafredo
9 Tasty Express
10 Tomato & Basil

VEGGIE FRIENDLY FOODS

11 Medicine Eatstation
12 Millenium

FREE FOOD!

13 The Big Four
   Restaurant
14 Dave's Bar
15 Escape From New
   York Pizza

FREE FOOD! (ctn'd)

16 The Holding
   Company
17 Macarthur Park
18 Morton's Steakhouse
19 Palio D'Asti
20 Perry's
21 Schroeders
22 The White Horse
   Pub

LATE NITE EATS

23 Cafe Mason
24 Lori's Diner

DRINKS DRINKS DRINKS

25 The Gold Dust
   Lounge
26 The Tonga Room
27 Ponzu

OUT

Wright

m

's

more

you to
Africa

nt your

Chinatown

Walking down Stockton Street, one's senses are assaulted with so many foreign smells and sights that it can be jarring. Sometimes it's kinda like, "Where the hell am I and what is that smell?" Well buddy, you're in Chinatown, and I don't know what the smell is either. Chinatown has two main streets: Grant, which is the tourist drag, and Stockton, which is where all of Chinatown's residents do their daily tasks like shopping and eating. Grant Street is full of stores that sell ornamental swords, t-shirts, calligraphy sets, slippers, Mao memorabilia, little license plates with every single name except Stuart, and hundreds of little toys that beep, buzz and whirr. Stockton is full of shops that sell fish, poultry, turtles, sharks, herbs for Chinese medicine, pastries, dried seahorses, crazy shit, clothes, Nike shoes and other daily essentials. Keep one thing in mind: the prices in Chinatown are generally really cheap and many of them are negotiable. The only problem is that a lot of people there don't speak English despite living in San Francisco for decades, and this can make the negotiations a little frustrating. Also know this: walking through Chinatown is like riding a bicycle in a swimming pool—don't expect to get anywhere too quickly. And while boarding the bus, watch out for old Chinese ladies because they will stop at nothing to get in front of you (I've been elbowed in the gut on numerous occasions).

This place has lots of Chinese people.

vorites simply because it is so damn good. They make all sorts of pastries and cakes with fruits and custards, and you can either get a pre-made, personal-sized one or a custom made big one. And they're really inexpensive for the quality you get.

Chinatown Restaurant
700 Washington St. @ Grant St.

Despite having the least creative name in the history of restaurant names, the Chinatown Restaurant happens to reside in one of the cooler looking buildings in the neighborhood. They also have a really aggressive marketing campaign that consists of one lady standing across the street handing out flyers. If you show any interest at all, she will stop at nothing to convince you to go into the restaurant. In fact, she followed me all the way in and up to the second floor just to make sure I made it. My only comment is that she deserves a raise because she is doing one hell of a job; the place was teeming with tourists. I wasn't even hungry, and I almost got some food just so I could get this lady to leave me alone. The food here looked really good and wasn't badly priced. And as an added note, according to the flyer, both Leonardo DiCaprio and former Governor Gray Davis have eaten there.

Dol Ho Restaurant
808 Pacific St. @ Stockton St.

This traditional sit down dim sum restaurant is perfect for a group of people. The food is pretty good, as are the prices, and if you order a bunch of stuff for a bunch of people, it ends up being not too expensive. If you are too busy to sit down for dim sum, Dol Ho does dim sum to go.

Gold Mountain
644 Broadway @ Stockton St.

This giant place has been holding it down in the SF dim sum scene for years. They have a devoted following and really good, affordable food. My parents turned me on to this place because it's their favorite dim sum spot in the City. Dim sum might be the most evolved style of eating I've ever seen; fuck getting up for the buffet—the buffet comes to you. The only thing that could top it might be the little sushi boats. That shit is just genius.

Good Luck Café & Deli
621 Kearny St. @ Sacramento St.

This spot's slogan is, "Any kind of sandwich without avocado and cheese for $3.80 + tax." Now that's savvy advertising—no slick shit like "best sandwich in town," these cats are just telling it like it is. Come in and hang out with all the old-timers who probably eat there every single day.

House of Nan King
919 Kearny St. @ Columbus St.

If you can't tell by all the awards on the walls, this place is really good. For some people, the House of Nan King is part of every trip to San Francisco. Although the prices have gone up in recent years, whatever you get is bound to be plentiful and tasty (and if you are not sure what to order, just ask the guy—he'll order for you). Make sure you get their wonton appetizer; it is the bomb.

Oishi
1199 Stockton St. @ Pacific St.

This little clean-looking, pseudo-outdoor corner spot has so many tasty inexpensive things that it's hard for me to pass by without getting something. To begin with, all their sandwiches are $1.95, and this includes anything from a ham sandwich to peanut butter and jelly to a mini pizza. Then they have the $1.00 Delicious

Sam Wo's

813 Washington St. @ Stockton St.

From what I understand, Sam Wo's used to be famous for having the most notoriously rude waiter in the world. Although he is now gone, his successors are definitely trying their best to follow the tradition. In fact, the surliness and utter indifference of the wait staff actually adds to the ambience of the restaurant. Sam Wo's is a really cool, funky place where you walk in through the kitchen, sit on one of the small upper levels, and the food comes upstairs by a dumb waiter (a system of levers and pulleys, not a waiter who can't talk) from the kitchen. The food is ridiculously cheap and decent tasting, and best of all, the restaurant is open until 3 a.m. every day except Sunday. If you can, I recommend sitting by the window on the third floor; it has a really neat view.

Uncle's Restaurant

65 Waverly St. @ Clay St.

This sparsely decorated, well-priced eatery is quite popular with Chinatown locals. The food here is pretty good, won't give you a stomach ache, and is of course, available for take out. The best deals are the Deluxe Family Dinners, where you and a few others can get a gang of food for as little as $8.95 a person.

Vietnam Deli Sandwich

Broadway @ Columbus Ave.

This place rides the line between North Beach and Chinatown so we'll just say it is in the latter. Like so many Vietnamese restaurants, this place sells good, cheap, big sandwiches as well as pho and noodles. My favorite is the barbecued chicken that is pretty filling and less than $3. Since it is open late, this is a great place to go once you've knocked a few back in North Beach.

You's Dim Sum

675 Broadway @ Stockton St.;
also 937 Stockton St. @ Clay St.

I don't know exactly what is on the menu at You's because it is all in Chinese, but I do know that like so many places in Chinatown it is *super* cheap. There is nothing on the menu for more than $2.50; and actually, most of it costs far less than that. You's is often teeming with people (which is always a good sign), and their pot stickers are of a freakishly huge size.

I'm going to say this in the most plain and honest way I can: I'm pretty sure Candy, the bartender here, is Dionysus disguised as a human being. It's the only logical way to explain the way she handles the position of bartender. It totally makes sense if you read any Greek mythology: gods used to come down to Earth in human form and just fuck around all the time. Look, if you're planning to go into the Bow Bow and only have one drink, just don't go, because I guarantee you will have more than one drink. It's almost like she's using a Jedi mind trick on you. And then once you've gotten nice and toasty and plan on leaving because you don't want to spend any more money, or you're too drunk, Candy starts *giving* you drinks! Sure I can sit here and talk about how the place is kinda grungy and smoky and the karaoke sounds like a siren PMS-ing, but the heart of the matter is this: Candy is the god of wine and debauchery incarnated into human form. If you don't believe me, go see for yourself.

Buddha Bar

901 Grant St. @ Washington St.

I don't know if you can get a better sign than the one this bar has; in fact, the sign is probably the best part of the place. It's simple but classic: red neon letters spelling out "Buddha" with a perfect neon martini glass next to it. The bar itself is small and on any given night the crowd ranges from Chinatown locals to young hipsters to piss drunk tourists. There are no frills here, just some people drinking and a really cool sign. That's it.

Grassland

905 Kearny St. @ Jackson St.

Even though the awning says, "Where good friends and girls meet," the closest thing to a girl that you are going to find in Grassland is a drunk 50-year-old woman. Despite the false advertising, this little Chinatown dive is a decent place to get a cheap, strong drink and hear some wild-ass stories from the bar's regulars. Drunk old men have some really crazy stories.

Li-Po Lounge

916 Grant St. @ Jackson St.

One of the few Chinatown bars whose patrons are not solely Chinese, the Li-Po Lounge is a very unique place. There are two

The Li-Po Lounge is kinda like a music video for some indie-rock band you've never heard of.

levels—the top is a bar with plenty of Chinese cultural paraphernalia, and the downstairs is a cavern-like basement used for throwing parties like the 80's night that happens every Friday. The drinks are pretty tiny for what you pay, but *goddamn* are they strong. Don't underestimate what you're drinking, or you will end up puking. Also you can rent out the downstairs for parties and it's pretty cheap.

...with so many stores selling cheap, shitty products, it's hard to choose just which one to shop at. I decided to put Canton Bazaar in here because it's the biggest. That's really the only thing that differentiates it from any of the other crap-dealing stores on Grant Street. So go buy yourself a Mao figurine, a jade Buddha and some poppers (no, not amyl nitrate).

Chinatown Kites
717 Grant St. @ Sacramento St.

I always hated kites as a kid. The amount of energy spent trying to get one of those fuckers in the air compared to the amount of enjoyment one receives from it being there just didn't do it for me. But then again there are a lot of people who have more patience than I do, and for those people there is Chinatown Kites. Here you can find everything from traditional Chinese silk kites to plastic Spiderman ones. It's kinda a neat place—if you like kites, that is.

K&A Boutique
800 Stockton St. & Sacramento St.

This one is for the ladies ... and the guys who like to wear ladies' clothing. K&A has amazingly stylish clothes at amazingly inexpensive prices. My ex-girlfriend was mad at me for some reason one time and in an effort to cool her down I bought her a really nice blouse at K&A. She thought that I'd spent like $80 on her when in actuality, it only cost me around $20. I guess now she'll be mad that I blew up this secret little shopping spot. Oh well.

Vital Tea-Leaf
1044 Grant St. @ Jackson St.

I'm putting this one under shopping because, technically speaking, this is a teashop. I don't actually expect you to buy tea here because it's absurdly overpriced. That being said, as your attorney, I advise you to stop into Vital Tea-Leaf and do some free tea drinking. They have this whole setup where you go in and taste a whole bunch of teas for free. Sure they totally push the teas on you afterwards, but there is no obligation to buy. Cool, right? Plus they have all these specialty teas for things like back pain, colds and herpes. Okay, I made that last one up.

Sights & Entertainment

This lovely and ornate building (which may actually be a different bank by now) once housed the Chinese Telephone Exchange, where Chinatown's first public telephone switchboard was operated. Although the CTE was first opened in 1891, this particular building was constructed after the 1906 earthquake. In an article I read about this spot on www.sfmuseum.org, the manager of the CTE in 1901 is quoted as saying they would have liked to have had all women switchboard operators because they have a better temperament. At the time of the interview though, they hadn't begun using women operators because it would cost too much to purchase them and bring them in from China ... WOW! I don't even know what to say about that.

Chinese Historical Society of America
965 Clay St. @ Stockton St.

Did you know that the United States has a long history of racism? No way! Who would've thought? Well guess what? You can learn all about yet another dim spot in our country's history, the persecution of Chinese immigrants, at this great museum. Of course it's not just about repression—the museum has all kinds of exhibits about the history of Chinese-Americans. Given the history of San Francisco, it makes a lot of sense that the oldest and largest organization concerned with studying and documenting Chinese-American history is in the City. With so many other more famous museums in SF, this excellent one often gets overlooked. But that's too bad because it is in an absolutely lovely building and is tremendously interesting. Admission is $3 or $2 with a student ID. Also, it's free on the first Thursday of the month.

The Golden Gate Fortune Cookie Factory
56 Ross Alley @ Grant St.

Chinatown is full of crazy shit, it really is. One of these is the Golden Gate Fortune Cookie Factory. Located on Ross Alley, you can go into this shop and see how fortune cookies are made. If you're lucky you might even get a little sample, but I doubt it. You can also buy bags of fortune cookies; in fact bring a bag of fortune cookies to the next potluck you go to. People will either think that you're creative or that you robbed Panda Express.

Portsmouth Square
Kearny St. between Clay & Washington Sts.

For many of San Francisco's early years, Portsmouth Square was the major focal point for all-important happenings in the City. It was here in 1848 that Sam Brannan announced that gold had been found in the Sierras. It was also here in 1859 where a eulogy was given over the body of U.S. Senator David C. Broderick who was killed in a pistol duel by Chief Justice David S. Terry. How fucking gangster is that? A judge and a senator settling a dispute with gunfire! Who needs filibusters? The square is named after the U.S.S. Portsmouth, which carried Captain John Montgomery to the Bay in 1846 so that he could claim California for the U.S. Today, it is one of the social centers for the residents of Chinatown. Any day of the week you can find children enjoying the playground, adults chatting while sitting on benches, or old folks gambling on Mah Jong and card games. Also, underneath the square is a big underground parking structure.

This woman is far better at making fortune cookies than I'll ever be at anything in my life. Photo by Trisha Gum

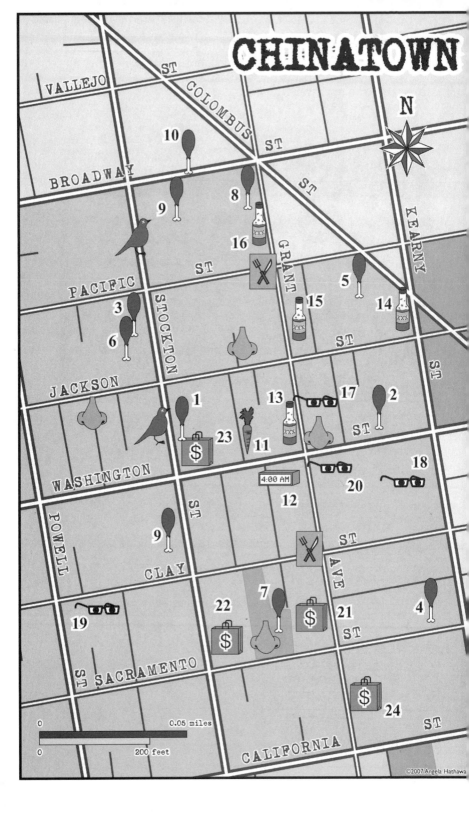

CHINATOWN

GRUB & PUB BIT...

[obscured text]

...? COLD MOUNTAIN

VEGGIE FRIENDLY FOODS

11 Lucky Creation

`4:00 AM` LATE NITE EATS

12 Sam Wo's

DRINKS DRINKS DRINKS

13 Buddha Bar
14 Grassland
15 Li-Po Lounge
16 Bow Bow Cocktail Lounge

👓 PLACES TO CHECK OUT

17 The Golden Gate
   Fortune Cookie Factory
18 Portsmouth Square
19 Chinese Historical
   Society of America
20 Bank of Canton

SHOPPING

21 Chinatown Kites
22 K&A Boutique
23 Vital Tea Leaf
24 Canton Bazaar

Dead animals in windows

Unidentifiable smells

Relentless menu hander-outers

The Sunset

The Sunset is more or less the area west of Stanyan and south of Golden Gate Park. I can't figure out why, but most of the people who live out here (especially the area east of 19th Avenue called the Inner Sunset) absolutely fucking love it. Some say it's because there is always parking, others say they are just excited to be living in a house, while others argue that their rent is actually cheaper than some of the other parts of the City. Being one of the foggier neighborhoods in San Francisco, this area was named the Sunset District in the 1880s by developer Aurelius E. Buckingham in order to trick people into buying some of the homes he had recently built. Just like the Richmond, the Sunset was mostly sand dunes until the early part of the twentieth century. Some of the first people to populate the area were the students of the University of California's medical school (now UCSF), which opened in the early 1900s. In recent decades, the Sunset has become an enclave for people from all over Asia and the Pacific Islands, making the Sunset a great place to get good, inexpensive meals from all over the world. In terms of shopping and nightlife, the area surrounding 9th Ave. and Irving has become a hot spot for trendy boutiques as well as upscale dining and bars.

Sunset = Foggy!!!

W. of Stanyan /S. of G.G.P.

UCSF

Sand Dunes but then developed by Aurelius E Buckingham in 1880's

Asian food... yummy

9th + Irving

Tiled steps → 16th + moraga

kinda fucking boring

... exactly like what you would imagine an organic café would look like: bright colors, plants, and other general funky decorations. The only major drawback of this place is that it's closer to Japan than it is to downtown San Francisco.

JJ Ice Cream
1152 Irving St. @ Funston St.

This little hole in the wall ice cream parlor is a perfect place to stop when you've been walking around the Sunset all day doing research for a Broke-Ass Guide. There is really not much to speak of in terms of interior design, but the ice cream (like all ice cream) is delicious. They also sell handmade purses, candy and other various tchotchkes (that's Yiddish for "knick-knacks"). A single scoop of ice cream is $1.75. This is the only price that has gone down since I started doing this guide thingy that I do.

Johnny's Hamburgers
2305 Irving St. @ 24th Ave.

Johnny's is just a cheap fucking hamburger place. It ain't pretty in there, but you can get a burger, fries and a soda for $5.50. What more do you want?

Kiki
1269 9th Ave. @ Irving St.

This place has ridiculously cheap sushi that is actually pretty good. You can get a five piece rock n' roll and six pieces of nigiri for $7.99. The interior here is also pretty cool because they have stills from different Anime films (not that I've seen any of them).

Lime Tree
450#A Irving St. @ 5th Ave.

This joint has very lime-colored walls, good cheap food and a super accommodating staff. The bomb-ass corn fritters are only $3.50 and nothing on the menu is over $6.99. All these things make me very happy and make it much easier to tolerate the awful smooth jazz on the stereo.

Little Bangkok
845 Irving St. @ 10th Ave.

The smallness of this Thai restaurant gives it a cozy feeling, but apart from the minimal carved woodwork, the inside is a little sparse. That's cool though because the food is good and well priced (most things are $7.95 or less), and the service is quick and friendly. I personally like that their outside sign is the type of fading 7-Up marquee usually reserved for corner liquor stores.

Naan 'n Curry
642 Irving St. @ 7th Ave.; *also* at 533 Jackson St. @ Columbus; 690 Van Ness Ave. @ Turk St.; and 336 O'Farrell St. @ Mason St.

If you love Indian/Pakistani food or are Indian/Pakistani-food-curious, this is the place for you. Naan 'n Curry is one of the true gems in this City (and in this guide). When I started doing this thing there were only one or two, and now it seems like they are slowly taking over the world. When I lived in the area, I frequented the Tenderloin spot (which is now open 24/7) at least twice a week and always got the Chicken Tikka Masla ($5.99) and a naan ($1). Go there and eat; you will thank me for it.

Peasant Pies
1039 Irving St. @ 12th Ave; *also* 4108 24th St. @ Castro St.

For me, the word "pie" has always followed such ~~~~~

Pluto's
627 Irving St. @ 8th Ave.;
also at 3258 Scott St. @ Lombard St.

The food at Pluto's tastes better than what they serve at the shoe repair place.

Taking the classic American idea of a cafeteria and giving it a quasi-corporate spin, Pluto's serves hearty fresh food at reasonable prices. Nothing on the menu is more than $6.50, but because it's cafeteria style and you can see all the tasty looking food, you get tricked into buying more than you actually need. (This is where I shake my fist, grimace, and say, "You bastards!") The food here is actually pretty good, and the salads are huge. If you buy more than you can eat, you can always take it home.

Sunrise Deli
2115 Irving St. @ 23rd Ave.

An island of Mediterranean food surrounded by an ocean of Asian restaurants, Sunrise Deli has quite possibly the best falafel, shawarma and kebabs in the whole city. They also sell a variety of Middle Eastern foodstuffs and baked goods, and to top it off they sell hookahs for $65 (which is probably cheaper than your stoner roommate who works at a head-shop on Haight can get them for).

Tel Aviv Kosher Meats Deli & Liquor
2495 Irving St. @ 25th Ave.

Are you having houseguests from Crown Heights, Brooklyn or West LA and don't have a single thing in your house that meets their dietary restrictions? Never fear! Lucky for you there's a kosher deli in the Outer Sunset. How good does a hot pastrami sandwich sound right now?

Yum Yum Fish
2181 Irving St. @ 23rd Ave.

This fish market/sushi joint is crazy inexpensive: a California Roll is only $2.50, and its devoted following makes getting a seat at one of the four tables a bit difficult. The faded posters of different fish make the place seem a little worn and might make you wary of eating here, but your first bite will dispel any reservations.

This is David over at Yum Yum Fish. The t-shirt underneath his robe says, "Sushi making motherfucker". He never wears t-shirts that lie.

Bars

...ng bar make it an inviting place,
while the outside smoking patio's retractable awning makes it
perfect for whatever the weather gods throw your way. The crowd
is a mix between middle-aged Sunset denizens and students from
nearby UCSF. In a way, the Blackthorn tavern is the type of place
you walk away from wishing it was just a little closer to your
house so you could go there more often.

Eagle's Drift In Lounge
1232 Noriega St. @ 19th Ave.

This is definitely one of those bars that you walk into and say to
yourself, "Where the fuck am I? There is no way I'm still in San
Francisco". This is a real dive bar, like on some Bukowski shit.
People go here to drink their lives away or alternatively, to play
darts and pool and watch people drink their lives away. The decor
is that of any shithole bar USA, sprinkled with little strange touches like giant black and white photos of Victorian-era drunks, year
round blinking x-mas lights and random eagle (like the actual
bird) paraphernalia. Apparently, there is some type of big pool
tourney that goes on here too.

Fireside Bar
603 Irving St. @ 7th Ave.

Guess why they named this the Fireside Bar? Because they have
a fireplace, dummy! This is not necessarily super cheap, but it's
a really nice place to spend an evening hanging out and talking

around the fire. The lighting and interior design really comple-
ment the vibe that the fireplace creates, and the patrons are the
upwardly mobile yet very friendly type. It's the kind of bar that
your friend who just moved out to the Sunset calls you about and
says, "Hey, I just found this really neat bar right by my house. It
even has a fireplace!"

Grandma's Saloon
1016 Taravel St. @ 20th Ave.

Grandma's clientele mostly consists of old people, poolsharks and
pukers. Patches from police, firemen and paramedics line the wall
behind the bar while an old mid-80's video game keeps a silent
vigil over a dismal scene. I hope I'm not drinking in places like
Grandma's in 30 years. It's almost more depressing than the dive
bars in the Tenderloin because it feels like these people decided
to be here while the folks in Loin just seem like they were born
into it. The woman behind the bar actually slid my ID into a card
reader to make sure I was 21, which was funny considering I was
26 and rocking a full beard. Maybe it's called Grandma's because
they expect you to be over 65. Regardless, a guy who looked like
he might be Grandpa was nodding off; sleeping upright in a chair
next to the pool table ... maybe he was dead.

The Little Shamrock
807 Lincoln St. @ 9th Ave.

When I finally came to The Little Shamrock for a drink I was a
little disappointed in myself for not having hung out here before.
On most nights of the week it's a chill spot to play some chess or
board games and knock back a few pints. And then on weekend
nights, the vibe changes and it gets crowded and rowdy and it's
a fun place to talk some shit and throw some darts. They even
have a whole backroom devoted to darts (between you and me,
I wanna get really good at darts and walk around with some
strapped to my arm so I can do some ninja shit like kill flies or
take motherfuckers' eyes out). Because The Little Shamrock is

one of the oldest bars in the city, they have all kinds of neat old stuff on the walls like stained glass windows and a clock that hasn't ticked since the 1906 earthquake. And the best part of the

⎯y ⎯ ⎯⎯ ⎯⎯ ⎯⎯⎯ ⎯⎯ ⎯⎯ ⎯⎯ guy bar-

hounds and cute young things. It has a real "regulars" type of feel to it; like you know the guy with the beard and the Giants cap has been there since opening time, but everyone there always seems to be in a good mood and more than welcoming. Some people come because you can watch sports and smoke inside, while others come for the pool table and good jukebox. Me, I went to do research and have a couple of strong, moderately priced drinks.

Yancy's Saloon
434 Irving St. @ 9th Ave.

The vibe of this place is kinda like a mixture between a sports bar, a dive bar and an Irish pub. Since it's a pretty large place it's great for those nights when you have a lot of people going out with you. For example, I've done the Broke-Ass Stuart pub crawl two years in a row so far (imagine a school bus and a trolley filled with people), and we've hit Yancy's both times because it was big enough to contain us. Both the prices and the drinks are average, but the crowd is usually fun, and a little rowdy. If you can, try to get one of the couches—they are nice and comfy.

Shopping

Archangel Bookstore
1352a 9th Ave. @ Judah St.

Although I have no great love for organized religion, I do have to admit that Eastern Orthodox Christianity is responsible for some really incredible artwork. The Archangel Bookstore has all kinds of neat Byzantine art, books, icons, crosses and imports. Then there's the miscellaneous stuff like the holy honey that my friend bought here. What the hell makes honey holy anyway?

Jazz Quarter
1267 20th Ave. @ Irving St.

If you like jazz, this record shop is either your wet dream or one of the most frustrating experiences you'll ever have. First of all, if it seems like this place is always closed, you might be right; it's only open from 1 to 6 p.m., Tuesday through Saturday. If by chance you are lucky enough to get there on a day when it is open, you'll be faced with mountains of music that might take millennia to sift through. That being said, there is an amazing amount of rare and out-of-print records here for you to discover. Also the owner is a super chill guy who is down to talk about jazz for forever, or at least for the five hours between 1 and 6 p.m.

Misdirections Magic Shop
1236 9th Ave. @ Lincoln St.

If you've ever wondered how to do card tricks, make smoke appear from your hands, or simply needed some high quality fake dog shit, then you should really go visit the people over at Misdirections. Considered Northern California's premier place for magicians' needs, this place does more than just sell gags and practical jokes. They even sponsor a lecture series that brings in some of the most respected magicians in the country. Here's a

place and that if you shop here all your dreams will be fulfilled. But it is a cool, funky shop, and my publisher felt that I needed to bulk up this section some, so Wishbone, you've made the cut (which I wouldn't be too proud of, considering that you're flanked by a fucking magic store). It's not my fault that the Sunset is pretty boring and there isn't much going on. Luckily, if you do want to get someone a gift that is almost useful enough and almost clever enough that it almost ceases to be kitschy, then you should shop at Wishbone. They've got a whole section devoted to Emily Strange gear, a bunch of Paul Frank clothing, and cute books, coasters and cards about shit like girls surfing and chocolate. Come to think of it, I like this store a lot.

Sights & Entertainment

The Canvas
1200 9th Ave. @ Lincoln St.

Despite being a restaurant and having a bar, this place falls into the entertainment category because the entertainment is the only inexpensive thing there. What's cool about The Canvas is that it's both an art gallery and a lounge, without having the overbearing pretension of other similar places in the City (111 Minna for example). The live entertainment at night is often free or only a couple bucks, and it ranges from open mics and jam sessions to local and touring bands. Another perk is that there are almost always hot people hanging out here.

The Ocean
The large body of water directly west of the City.

If you go out far enough, you're bound to hit this big, wet sonofabitch. It's cold, and there are really only like five days a year where the sun shines, but there are bonfire pits, so if you feel up to making the trek, you can make some delicious s'mores.

The Tiled Steps
16th Ave. @ Moraga St.

This is a really lovely mosaic running up the 163 steps at 16th Ave and Moraga. There are all kinds of fishies and suns and moons going on. It's pretty cool to look at, and if you're not too lazy, I bet the view from the top is pretty rad. I was too lazy.

The San Francisco Zoo

Sloat Blvd. @ 47th Ave.

It's a motherfucking zoo. They've got animals. It's

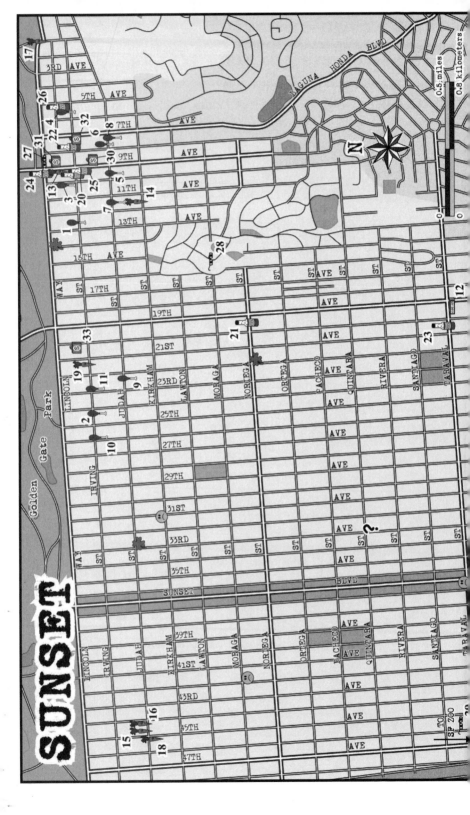

SUNSET

GRUB-A-DUB-DUB

1 JJ Ice Cream
2 John's Hamburgers
3 Kiki
4 Lime Tree
5 Little Bangkok
6 Naan 'n Curry
7 Peasant Pies
8 Pluto's
9 Sunrise Deli
10 Tel Aviv Kosher Meats Deli & Liquor
11 Yum Yum Fish

LATE NITE EATS

12 JT's (Island Cafe)

VEGGIE FRIENDLY FOOD

13 Daily Health Food & Deli
14 Enjoy Vegetarian Restaurant
15 Feel Real Organic Cafe
16 Judahlicious
17 New Ganges Restaurant
18 Other Avenues Food Store
19 Shangri-La

DRINKS DRINKS DF

20 Blackthorn Ta
21 Eagle's Drift-
22 Fireside Bar
23 Grandma's Salc
24 The Little Sha
25 Mucky Duck
26 Yancy's Saloon

PLACES TO CHECK (

27 The Canvas
28 The Tiled Step:
29 SF Zoo

SHOPPING

30 Archangel Book
31 Misdirections l
32 Wishbone
33 Jazz Quarter

? The middle of fuck

☺ Person who is supe
live in the Sunset

☘ Irish people not n

Golden Gate Park

G olden Gate Park is 1,017 acres of a good time. In fact it is 174 acres more of a good time than Central Park in New York. And guess what? Most of it is free. Feel like smoking a bowl and playing Frisbee? Head to the park. Wanna go for a jog and not have to dodge Dodges (or to be honest, Mini Coopers)? GGP is your place. Your old lady kicked you out and you can't afford a hotel room? Nobody has to pay to sleep in the park! If you can't figure out what to do with wide-open green spaces and free time, I'm not gonna spell it out for you. But what I am gonna do is tell you about some of the specific attractions that you can go to when you're tired of laughing at 17-year-old kids on mushrooms who are rolling around in the foliage and yelling that they've made some profound discoveries about the universe. Some are free and some cost money; it's up to you to decide which ones you want to visit. I can only take you so far.

Conservatory of Flowers: Opened in 1879, this lovely example of a Victorian-era greenhouse is one of the oldest and most visited attractions in Golden Gate Park. I'm not much of a plantologist (I barely even eat vegetables), so I'm not gonna sit here and talk a bunch of guff about something I know nothing about. I do have one great recommendation though—go to the Conservatory of Flowers on a really cold day. Because so many of the plants come from tropical regions, they keep the greenhouse hot and humid. So when it's rainy and miserable in the middle of February, you can go and pretend you're in Bali. In fact, you should totally wear a big heavy coat with a swimsuit underneath, bring a magazine and a folding chair and pretend you're sitting out on the beach. See how long it takes them to kick you out. This plant palace is free on the first Tuesday of the month. Otherwise it costs $5 or $3 with a student ID.

Japanese Tea Garden: Built in 1894 for a World's Fair called the California Midwinter International Exposition, the Japanese Tea Garden is the oldest public Japanese Garden in the U.S. The five-acre garden is a favorite of locals and tourists alike because of its beautiful landscaping, yummy tea and its tranquility. (Although how tranquil can it be with tons of tourists snapping photos?) Last time I checked, admission was just $3.50. All I know is that motherfuckers seem to love this place.

The de Young Museum: Just recently reopened in 2005 after years of remodeling, the de Young Museum is an architectural masterpiece as well as a home to an immense amount of world-class art. The museum is known for its collections of African and Oceanic art as well as its hefty amount of work by American painters. But really, the one thing I will always remember the de Young for (hazily of course) is its opening weekend party. The first night of the opening was for the mayor and the blue-blooded socialites who donated money to the restoration. Needless to say, the only broke-asses allowed were the ones working there. The following night though they opened the museum up for free for

31 hours and had a real fucking party. There was live music, DJs, dance performances and if I remember correctly (which I doubt), there were even fire dancers. When we arrived very intoxicated

ing the art. My roommate Jeremy was so drunk that he asked me to slap him across the face a few times to try and wake him up. I generously obliged and then put him in a cab and sent him home. It was about 6:30 a.m. by the time I got into bed. It was easily one of my favorite nights in San Francisco. Anyway, back to business. The museum costs $10 and $6 with a student ID. Admission includes entrance to the big-ass tower that has a view of most of SF. The first Tuesday of the month is free, but you still have to pay to see the special exhibit.

San Francisco Botanical Garden at Strybing Arboretum: 9th Ave. @ Lincoln St.

These 55 acres of pretty stuff are open and free every day of the year. They even offer free walking tours if you really want to spend your day getting talked to about 7,000 varieties of plants (count me out). The garden itself officially opened in 1940, only to be drafted into the army three years later. It survived the war but lost an eye at Normandy. (What else do you want me to say about a bunch of plants?)

Stowe Lake: Nothing gets the ladies going like a little row boating on Stow Lake ... oh yeah! I only know this because the one girl I brought there, I've been stuck with ever since (just kidding, I love you, honey. Don't make me sleep on the couch tonight). But seriously, this is a great spot for a date because you can rent a little boat ($14 per hour), do some rowing around and then eat a little ice cream. If that's not romantic, then I must be watching the wrong movies. Isn't it ridiculous which things we're conditioned to think are romantic? I feel there's a lot of people being let down out there because the bar is set way too high by movies, TV and books, and people really believe that shit. I mean really, *Dirty Dancing* and *Pretty Woman*? That's what we're supposed to live up to? You've got to be kidding me. (I think I officially just ensured that I'm never going to get laid again).

Hippie Hill: Just past where the Haight runs into the park, Hippie Hill is the place to go on a sunny day if you just wanna get stoned and chill out. Every Saturday you can find a drum circle there, and if you are looking to buy drugs from strangers (which I almost never advise) this is your spot. The joke is that if you're buying weed on Haight or in the park you're getting a "Haith" instead of an eighth because it's gonna be short. Regard-less, Hippie Hill can be a fun place to spend a few hours because it's one of the best weirdo watching spots in the world.

The Marina

Going out in the Marina at night is a lot like going to a frat party. All the guys have on the same striped shirts and call each other Bro, while all the girls have streaked blonde hair, skimpy dresses and cleavage. Not that all this is necessarily a bad thing (especially the cleavage), it's just that it gives the Marina a real generic feel. If you are looking to find a dreamy young Republican then this is the perfect neighborhood for you. In the daytime the Marina is one of the City's main high-end shopping districts, where you can buy clothes made by hard to pronounce designers, and eat at whatever type of fusion restaurant is currently hot. What is actually interesting about the Marina though is that it is primarily built on landfill. The Marina was more or less created for the Panama-Pacific International Exposition and after the Expo was dismantled people began moving to this new and beautiful part of town. Unfortunately, because it was built on a landfill, the Marina was one of the areas struck hardest during the 1989 Loma Prieta Earthquake, causing many a building to crumble to the ground.

Food

Askew Grill

3348 Steiner St. @ Chestnut St.; *also* 1607 Haight St. @ Clayton St.; and 3538 16th St. @ Market St.

Consistently rated as one of the City's best cheap and healthy food spots, Askew skewers up bomb-ass barbequed meats, seafood and veggies and puts them on a bed of starches or salad. The BBQ sauce here is absolutely delicious as are the mashed potatoes and the corn. But the true gem here is the nachos. Unfortunately, they may not always make them for you, so you will have to ask very nicely. In fact, they may only have them at the Haight location, so I'm not making any promises. Actually, uh, never mind about the nachos.

Barney's Gourmet Hamburgers

3344 Steiner St. @ Chestnut St.;
also 4138 24th St. @ Castro St.

Barney's has a ludicrous amount of burger choices, most of which can be a little expensive. But the basic Barney Burger is only $6.50, which isn't too bad considering the area. They also have gourmet milkshakes. What the fuck is a gourmet milkshake? What's next, a gourmet corndog? If you do eat at Barney's, try to sit in the back patio—it's very pretty.

All Star Donuts

2095 Chestnut St. @ Steiner St.

There are two remarkable things about this donut shop. The first is that it is probably the cheapest bite to eat in the Marina; a sandwich is only $3.50. The second thing is that it has an extremely cool, old neon sign. The sign is of a donut being dunked into a cup of coffee. I have a weird obsession with neon signs, especially old ones. I dig them because when you look at them at

it's also not one of the really upscale spots either. Your average plate here is gonna be like eight bucks, but it's fairly heaping in quantity. The thing that struck me the most though was that at the entrance they have this three-foot-tall, full-color statue of like the most minstrelized Chinese stereotype. Standing in a red and gold dragon dress gown, the statue has a little wispy mustache, giant buckteeth, little sandals and a serving tray, making the whole thing an awful reminder of how Asians used to be portrayed by American media. It's a strange statue to have.

The Grove

2250 Chestnut St. @ Pierce St.

I had spent the better part of an hour wandering around the Marina looking for a cheap bite, and this was the best I could do. The place is laid out nicely with a big woodsy theme going on, and the free WiFi kept people around long enough to make it seem busy. I also ran into two people I know there, but in both interactions, nobody asked the other what they were doing in the Marina. It's kind of like running into someone you know in the Planned Parenthood waiting room—it almost feels like there's some guilt attached to it. I ended up having an $8 sandwich that, while tasting good, was still $8. But at least it came with a pickle and some chips.

Home Plate
2274 Lombard St. @ Pierce St.

People love the hell out of this sparsely decorated Marina haunt. It's probably the completely unpretentious atmosphere or the fact that it is *so* well priced for how good it is. They have the coolest stuff for breakfast too, like banana-walnut buttermilk pancakes, blintzes with apricot-strawberry sauce and corn and bell pepper savory cakes (I'm not quite sure what the last one is, but it sounds good, doesn't it?). This place is a welcome relief from the other eateries in the neighborhood.

Johnny Rockets
2201 Chestnut St. @ Pierce St.

Fuck Johnny Rockets.

Marina Liquor and Deli
2299 Chestnut St. @ Scott St.

I feel like San Francisco is lacking in the liquor-and-deli depart-ment. But the Marina has this good one. Where else could you get a $5 sandwich, a Slim Jim and a 40? See, liquor-and-deli's are a very integral part of society. I wish I had one by my house. ☹

Marina Submarine
2299 Union St. @ Steiner St.

This is really just a sparse little shop that sells good sandwiches. It's like a better tasting Subway, and doesn't have Subway's weird, sickening smell. Most of the five-inch subs are under $5, except the Atomic Sub, which has more ingredients than I care to list. They also make sandwiches up to six-feet-long.

Original Buffalo Wings
2499 Lombard St. @ Divisadero St.

Have you ever tried to eat a whole bunch of Buffalo wings while sober? It's a pretty demanding task. We ordered the De La Hoya/

Mayorga fight on pay-per-view and for some ungodly reason we also decided to order 100 Buffalo wings. There were only four or five of us, but we figured that since we usually destroy a couple

like it!"

Osha Thai Noodle

Buchanan St., 149 2nd St. @ Minna St.

(see entry on page 53)

The Pita Pit

2257 Chestnut St. @ Avila St.

Who would have thought that a Canadian chain restaurant could actually make it all the way to San Francisco? The Pita Pit is a lot

like Subway, but healthier and with pitas instead of bread. Everything here is under $6.50, and the backside of the menu has the nutritional information for everything they've got. Does anyone know what the hell Souvlaki is? Well you can get a pita full of it here.

I have no clue why I took this photo.

Pizza Orgasmica

3157 Fillmore St. @ Greenwich St.

(see entry on page 106)

Pluto's

3258 Scott St. @ Lombard St.

(see entry on page 209)

$0.20 chicken wings on Wednesdays. Bar None is basically a frat party every night—they even have a beer pong table—and the only reason I've ever gone was because my friend who worked there hooked us up with drinks. I'm a pretty chill guy, but for some reason this place seems to be the only bar in the City where I come close to getting in a fight every time I go. Fuck this place; it belongs in Pacific Beach in San Diego.

The Bus Stop
1901 Union St. @ Laguna St.

Though I'm not sure when it became a sports bar, the Bus Stop started serving drinks way back in that wonderful year of 1900. I have a feeling that in those days the walls weren't covered in 49'ers memorabilia or in t-shirts signed by the likes of Bill Clinton and Monica Seles. I bet that in 1900 the Bus Stop didn't sell shots of Jägermeister for $3.50 on Saturday nights and $3.50 Captain Morgan's drinks on Mondays. I'd also wager that this watering hole didn't have TVs broadcasting Major League Baseball games back then either. But then again, I could be wrong.

City Tavern
3200 Fillmore St. @ Greenwich St.

The only times I really go to this place are when I have a cousin in town or someone else visiting who really wants to go to the Marina. It's got good specials every night, like $2 cheeseburgers, wings and beers on Tuesdays, and $3 SKYY vodka on Thursdays.

But there's a reason the nickname for this place is "Shitty Tavern"; it's generally packed with complete fuck-wads. Cheap drinks attract all kinds.

The Horseshoe
2024 Chestnut St. @ Fillmore St.

They like sports here enough to project them on a screen. That's cool, I like sports too. I also like the softball trophies above the bar. But what I really like is all the old black and white photos of San Francisco. My favorite is the one of the people sitting on Nob Hill, smiling and having a good ole time while watching downtown burning after the 1906 earthquake/fire. It's funny because they don't know that their houses are gonna be burnt down two days later. Ha Ha! Stupid Victorian-era people! I also learned a good way to get rid of hiccups from a bartender here: mix bitters, sugar and lemon juice in a shot glass and then drink it.

HIFI
2125 Lombard St. @ Fillmore St.

Red lighting, $4 Budweisers and a dance floor … could be worse. They have decent drink specials throughout the week, but otherwise stick to Bud and PBR because their well drinks are at least $6. The crowd can be hit or miss, and when I say "crowd", I mean it. This joint gets packed, especially on the weekends. But during the week there isn't a cover charge and best of all, Wednesday is Bingo night (hey I'm trying here, I can't fake enthusiasm).

The Mauna Loa Club
3009 Fillmore St. @ Union St.

So here's the skinny—this is one of those places that has the potential to be one of the best dives in the City, but then has one major shortcoming. The Good: the bartenders here are amazing at making drinks and being nice people; the interior looks like someone was going for a Hawaiian/Tiki theme, but then got lazy and gave up halfway through. (Note the giant turtle shell on the

wall ... awesome!) In the back they even have that basketball game that you used to play at Chuck

The guy who runs this joint bought my book back when it was a zine. That's awesome.

P.S. If you're a dude in a striped shirt, or a girl who complains about how uncomfortable your ridiculous shoes are, I still love you. Please buy my book.

Notte

1851 Union St. @ Laguna St.

This spot is laid out pretty poorly, so when it's packed it can be an unsightly mess, but given the neighborhood, that's really one of its only drawbacks (if you're a straight man, that is). The clientele of Notte is generally attractive blond girls in black dresses and older guys who are trying to fuck them. I seriously think that any guy whose game is better than, "I drive a Mercedes" could have a lovely time here. It took me a second to figure out why so many cute young things go here, and then I looked at the bar staff; they're all pretty boy surfer types. Anyway, the bar also has a decent jukebox, Pac-Man, a comfortable lounge area in the back and genuinely good art on the walls. All around, not a bad spot, unless your game really is, "I drive a Mercedes."

↓

Sights & Entertainment

The Exploratorium

3601 Lyon St. @ Jefferson St.

Easily the coolest museum in the City, this hands-on science museum was originally founded by Dr. Frank Oppenheimer, the main man with the atomic plan (he was famously the director of the Manhattan Project). The Exploratorium has nothing to do with atom bombs or nuclear power plants though; it's all about making science cool by demonstrating it through neato displays and experiments. I guess it still doesn't sound great does it? *Just shut the fuck up and go*! I promise you'll like it. It's free on the first Wednesday of the month, but considering how many greedy little kids are there that day, it's almost worth paying the $13 (yikes!) to go on another occasion.

Fort Mason

Marina Blvd. @ Buchanan St.

Once upon a time, Spanish soldiers lived here. After they left, U.S. soldiers moved in. Then the 1906 earthquake happened and regular citizens camped out for a bit while the City was rebuilt. Now art and culture live here. Oh yeah, and a bunch of stinky backpackers too. The art and culture that I'm talking about is the Fort Mason Center, which is home to 30-plus museums and nonprofit organizations. And the stinky backpackers I mentioned all stay at the Fort Mason Hostel. Go for a walk around Fort Mason and see some neat stuff.

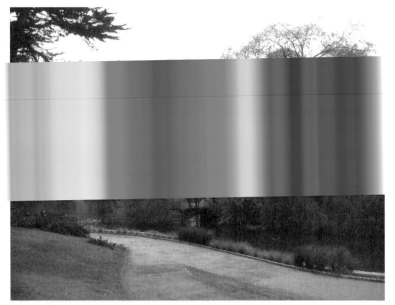

The Palace of Fine Arts is so pretty it's almost sickening.

Palace of Fine Arts

3601 Lyon St. @ Jefferson St.

Originally built for the 1915 Panama-Pacific International Exposition, a World's Fair of sorts, to celebrate the opening of the Panama Canal, the Palace of Fine Arts has come to be recognized as the crown jewel in a city full of architectural gems. Being the only building left from the Expo, this slightly dilapidated domed beauty sits on a pond often frequented by many ducks and swans. One time while I was there, I saw some stupid redneck chasing around a swan to impress his kids with his toughness. I didn't get to see how it ended, but I walked away hoping that the swan would bite the shit out of the man, teaching him not to bully little animals. Regardless of how that incident ended, I feel it would be remiss of me not to tell you that the Palace of Fine Arts also houses a 1,000 seat performing arts theatre that has been the venue for a 1976 Presidential debate, concerts ranging from Tori Amos to Tito Puente, and lectures by everyone from Timothy Leary to Henry Kissinger. The swans are not allowed inside.

The Wave Organ

The good people at the Exploratorium built the Wave Organ in
1986. It is made entirely of stones from a Gold Rush-era grave-
yard that got moved to make way for housing. The Wave Organ
is a bunch of tubes of various size sticking down through the
concrete, into the water, which make all sorts of neat sounds
depending on the height of the tide. It is an absolutely free thing,
but it does take a bit of walking. The best directions I got were
these: Walk along Marina Green heading west. Just before the entrance to the Bridge/Presidio, turn right and walk along the beach
towards the bay. When you get to the path that runs along the
bay and the yacht docks, follow the path out past the lighthouse
and keep going until you're there. Yeah, I know it sounds like a
treasure map from *The Goonies*, but follow the directions and you
will be very glad you did. If you're up all night, it's a great place to
watch the sunrise.

...rug ... west dtvit the
Bridge / Presidro, turn L. and
walk along beach towards Bay.
When you get to the path along
Bay and docks, follow path
past lighthouse and keep going

THE GOONIES

sounds like A treasure map

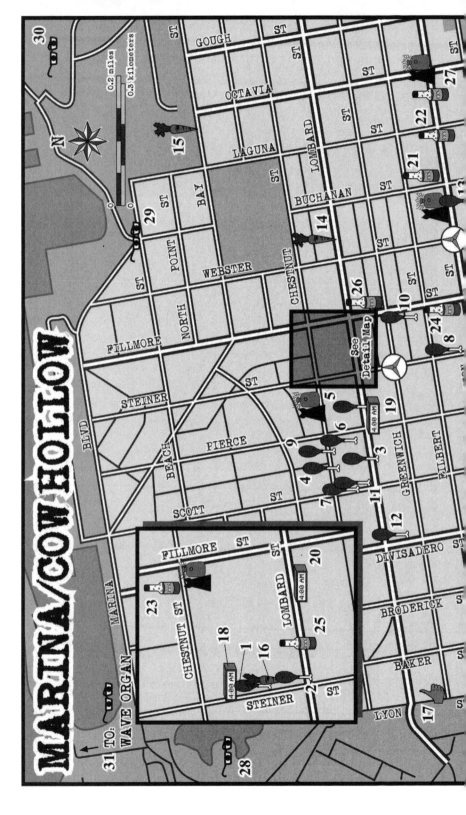

MARINA/COW HOLLOW

MARINA/ COW HOL[LOW]

GRUB-A-DUB-DUB

1 Askew Grill
2 Barney's Gourmet
   Hamburgers
3 Feng Shui
4 The Grove
5 Home Plate
6 Johnny Rockets
7 Marina Liquor and
   Deli
8 Marina Submarine
9 The Pita Pit
10 Pizza Orgasmica
11 Pluto's
12 Original Buffalo
   Wings
13 OSHA Thai Noodle
   House

VEGGIE FRIENDLY FOODS

14 Alive!
15 Greens
16 Lettus Cafe
   Organic

FREE FOOD!

17 Liverpool Lil's

LATE NITE EATS

18 All Star Donuts
19 IHOP
20 Mel's Diner

DRINKS DRINKS DRINKS

21 Bar None
22 The Bus Stop
23 The Horseshoe
24 The Mauna Loa
   Club
25 HI-FI
26 City Tavern
27 Notte

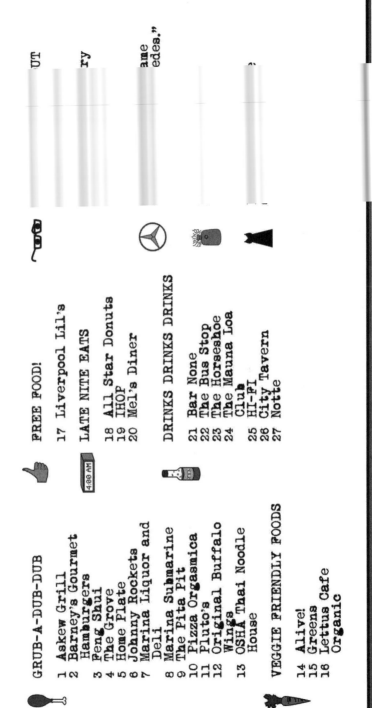

The Castro

I f San Francisco is the Mecca of the gay world, then the Castro is its Great Mosque. Every year thousands of Queer people from all over the world come to the Castro to see what it's like to be in a place where no one has to hide who they are or who they like to fuck. Although it is not exclusively gay, a staggering amount of the Castro's residents are, and because of this, many of the businesses are gay owned and cater to a largely gay clientele. But don't be intimidated if you're straight—the Castro is very straight friendly and many of the establishments are a nice mixture of both gay and not so gay. In fact, if you're a straight male the Castro is a great place to get an ego boost because gay men have no shame when it comes to checking people out. I know I always feel sexier when I'm in the Castro. If you are in San Francisco during the last weekend in June, you are in for a special treat—the Gay Pride celebration. It is a whole weekend of festivities with the highlights being the giant street party in the Castro on Saturday night and the Pride Parade down Market Street on Sunday.

Food

7-11
3998 18th St. @ Noe St.; also all over the nation

Sitting by yourself on the curb in front of 7-11 and eating their nachos at 5 a.m. is quite possibly the loneliest place on Earth. Trust me, I've been there. I don't know what it is about their nachos that make them such a wonderful guilty pleasure. Maybe it's the fact that the cheese and chili come from a machine that hums and dispenses as if it were giving out soft-serve frozen yogurt. Or maybe it's because of the time that I saw the machine opened and was able to look into the belly of the beast, where I found two plastic bags, one cheese and one chili, put through ringers that help squeeze out that sweet manna that makes you loathe yourself after eating it. Or maybe it's really the fact that Sevies, as we affectionately call it, is often the only 24-hour place in the area and sometimes you just have to make do with what you've got, even if it is the loneliest place in the world.

Bagdad Café
2295 Market St. @ 16th St.

I am not going to lie to you, this place is by no means cheap; it's not exactly expensive either, but I don't want you to be like, "That motherfucker Broke-Ass Stuart said his guide was all about living cheaply and dude is sending me to places with like nine dollar burgers and shit. Fuck him." The reason I'm including Bagdad Café is that the food is good, the portions are big, the servers are friendly and it's open 24 hours. And if you can get a seat by the window, you get to see all the madness going on outside, especially at three in the morning.

Castro Tarts
564 Castro St. @ 18ᵗʰ St.

1001 Market St. @ Octavia St.

Passing by this place at nighttime, I find it really hard to resist the allure of its tall neon sign. Looking at it, you almost have to wonder if somebody forgot to modernize just that one tiny half block; like maybe, if you step inside, it will actually be the 1940s and not whatever year it is now. But alas, it never is. The closest it comes is black and white photos on the walls and little jukeboxes at your table. The prices aren't exactly circa 1940 either, but that's a little too much to ask for I guess. If you have the hankering for some pancakes at 3 a.m., hit this place up; just don't try on Sunday, because they close at 11 p.m.

Jumpin Java
139 Noe St. @ Henry St.

Jumpin Java is a great place to get work done. They've got free WiFi, mellow background music and more electrical outlets than a marijuana grow room. In fact, since my girlfriend lived near here (and I was homeless and staying with her), I did a lot of work for this book here. Maybe in the future, when this writing shit has made me famous, and I die at a premature age, and my widow and my illegitimate children are squabbling over my millions because I didn't leave a will, and some genius has started city tours following the "Broke-Ass" path, people will come to this spot and say, "Wow, he really used to sit here and write!" Probably not, but the truly amazing thing about this place is that it might be the only spot in the world where you get this many gay men together and not a single person is picking up on anyone. Truthfully it's a little eerie.

No Name Sushi
314 Church St. @ 15th St.

I think this place really has no name, and if it does, the people who work here probably don't even know what it is. Here you can get a 16-piece roll for something like $5. Also like some other San Francisco spots, they don't serve drinks, so you are expected to bring your own, even if it's a brown bagged Mickey's 40 oz.

Orphan Andy's
3991 17th St. @ Castro St.

Yet another of the many Castro area 24-hour food spots. Orphan Andy's is a little place with pretty good food and pretty good prices. It has a kinda fun, retro-kitsch thing going on inside, and the staff is generally pretty nice and full of good, insightful conversation. One night I was there till four in the morning having one of those meaning-of-life-type conversations with a burnt-out tweeker, a sub-normal, impish 60-year-old Chinese man, and the server. It was enlightening, to say the least.

Quickly
415 Castro St. @ Market St.

Why aren't more businesses named with adverbs? Because it sounds silly, that's why. But silly sounding or not, this place is dirt-cheap. They have roughly 200 different drinks—mostly with tapioca pearls in them—all for fewer than three bucks; and their selection of fried finger foods is also plentiful and most of the stuff costs less than $3.99.

Rossi's Deli
426 Castro St. @ Market St.

In general, you can't really go wrong with a liquor and deli. Coffee by the pound, sandwiches for less than $5 and cheap cigarettes (if

I had a lawyer, this would be the part where I'd be asked to mention that Broke-Ass Stuart in no way endorses smoking—unless of course you are pregnant or underage)

jard thyme, when you're sliding into first and you feel a big fat burst, diarrhea, diarrhea"). Whether or not this place gives you diarrhea is completely out of my hands and has more to do with your digestive system than I care to know about. But I digress ... Sliders is a pretty good hamburger joint. A 6 oz burger is $3.75 and an 8 oz one is $4.50. They also let you choose from more than 20 condiments. I like avocado on my slider.

Sparky's Diner
242 Church St. @ Market St.

Although this restaurant is open 24 hours a day, the most exciting time to come is Thursday through Saturday after 2 a.m. Sometimes it seems that every person you have managed to converse with that night ends up there. Being in limbo between the Castro and the Mission, the crowd is about as mixed as can be. And for as busy as it gets, the servers are pretty cool and calm. For those of you trying to get laid and realizing the night is coming to an end, this place is as good as last chances get.

Woodhouse Fish Company
2073 Market St. @ 14th St.

If I were to make a song about how I feel today, the chorus would be, "I love seeaafooood!" followed, by some handclaps, some 808 drums and maybe even some synth horns. Yeah, that would be fresh! But not as fresh as the food at the Woodhouse. Damn this shit is good. Being a West Coast boy, I'd never had things like a

Lobsta (lobster) Roll or Steamers before, and now that I have, all I gotta say is, Stuie likes it! Granted I might be a little biased because I worked here for a while, and it's the best service industry job I've ever had (and I've had a lot). Now normally the prices are not exactly what you'd call broke-ass, but on Tuesdays, oysters are $1, half a crab is $7 and a pint of beer is $3. That's a good deal, right?

set up in a way that makes it easy to meet new friends while sitting around drinking. In fact, the couch set-up reminds me of certain theme tents at Burning Man. The mixed drinks here, while being well poured, are not the cheapest. But this is compensated for by the fact that they sell Pabst by the can, as well as Mickey's grenades. The amber lighting gives the place a smooth yet unpretentious vibe, and the old TV showing things like a very long loop of fish tank footage is awesome. If you're going to spend the $7 on a high-end mixed drink, try one of their specialties like the Raspberry Beret.

SF Badlands

4121 18th St. @ Castro St.

I actually worked here one summer as a bar back; I was the only straight guy there. And you know what's crazy? I could've gotten more ass from straight women while working there than if I'd been working at a non-gay bar (not that it mattered because I had a girlfriend at the time). But if you're a gay man looking for a little action, Badlands is the place to go. This meat market has TVs all over the place that play music videos for a very happening dance floor. The side effect of this is that now I can't hear anything off Justin Timberlake's first album without being reminded of sweaty gay guys rubbing against each other. Same goes for Beyonce's "Crazy in Love". Like most Castro bars, this joint has great drink specials all week long including a two-for-one happy hour and something called a "beer bust" on Sundays.

The Bar
456 Castro St. @ 18th St.

Plush silver padded walls, an elevated DJ booth, a disco ball and blaring Madonna music. I know it sounds like a lot of Castro bars, but what sets this one apart is that it's busy almost every night of the week. Although each night has great drink specials, the best time to go is Monday night when all well drinks are—get this—80 cents! Fucking crazy, right? They should hand out condoms with every third drink because, at that price, everyone should get drunk enough to end up going home with somebody.

The Café
2367 Market St. @ Castro St.

The Café is one of the better bars in the Castro because it has a good mix of both gay men and lesbians. The result of this seems to be a relatively drama-free zone, which everyone knows is a rare thing in the Castro. The drinks cost standard prices, the people are good-looking and if it is not too crowded, you can usually hear well enough to be able to socialize. The best part of this bar though is the second story patio that looks down onto Market Street.

The Edge
4149 18th St. @ Collingwood St.

If you like your men with beards, hairy chests and flannel shirts, then stop reading this book and go to The Edge now. Proclaiming itself to be San Francisco's "Bear Bar" for more than 15 years, this semi-cave-like spot has nightly drink specials, $3 Budweisers and a plethora of black and white photos involving leather and penises.

Lucky 13
2140 Market St. @ Church St.

One of the best dive bars in the City—cans of Pabst Blue Ribbon are only $2 all the time. They also have a little popcorn machine so you have something to munch on while you drink. If you get there before 11 p.m., you can even sit on the back patio (if you can find room). While you're there, if you have any extra scratch, pick up a Lucky 13 t-shirt or hoodie; they have a great logo. And best of all.

on the giant screens while knocking a few back. On the wall they have a schedule of which shows are played when, and which drink specials accompany which shows. Like on Sundays, you can watch *The Simpsons* and drink $2.25 well drinks. The best deal though is on Mondays, when from 2 p.m. to 2 a.m. all drinks are two-for-one. Whatever you order, they bring out two of them. Would you consider that to be the best happy hour ever, or just the most sadistic? My body hates me just for thinking about it.

The Mint

1942 Market St. @ Duboce St.

The Mint is definitely one of the most entertaining bars in San Francisco. This karaoke bar in the Castro district is a good mix of both gay and straight, and often you will see work or birthday parties. Remember, most people have to be pretty drunk to get up and sing, so you can see some pretty funny shit. There is nothing like seeing a 300-pound drag queen singing "You Make Me Feel Like a Natural Woman". It's kinda touching in a way.

The Mix

4086 18th St. @ Castro St.

A small neighborhood dive in the heart of the Castro, The Mix has awesome nightly drink specials, a pool table, some bench seating, a patio, a few lesbians and a lot of gay guys.

Moby Dick

4049 18th St. @ Hartford St.

Moby Dick has been considered one of most laid back bars in all of the Castro for over 25 years now. Of course it gets crowded on the weekends like any bar, but it is much more oriented towards hanging out, drinking and meeting people than it is towards dancing the night away. The drink specials here are ridiculous. Every day, margaritas are two for one, except on Sundays when Sex on the Beach is two for one. They also have a happy hour that goes from 3 until 8 p.m. The people at Moby Dick are always very friendly, and the big-ass fish tank above the bar is terrific.

Do you like to wear a feather boa and a tiara while fixing things around the house? (I know I do.) If so, then the fine people at Cliff's are waiting to help you find whatever you need. This is seriously one of the coolest places ever, and only in the Castro could you ever find anything like it. This giant hardware store sells everything from power drills to Swiss Knives to Halloween masks to DSL cables and Mad Libs. Even if you're not buying anything, you at least have to go in and see the place for yourself.

Get Lost Travel Books
1825 Market St. @ Guerrero St.

The second most exciting thing about traveling (behind actually traveling) is planning your trip, which is exactly where Get Lost comes in. For the past ten years or so, Get Lost has been supplying San Franciscans with guidebooks, maps, gear and sound travel advice. Besides being the owner of an independent travel store, Lee is also a traveler himself, which means that he's funneled his passion into helping make your trip better.

Under One Roof
549 Castro St. @ 19th St.

All of the profits that this adorably kitschy gift shop earns go directly to AIDS service organizations, making shopping here satisfying on every level. You can buy things like red velvet Buddhas, silly lamps, picture frames and San Francisco/Castro paraphernalia. It's like shopping in the entry section of Urban Outfitters, except that the money is going to something benefiting the world, instead of to someone who's trying to capitalize on your nostalgia.

Worn Out West

582 Castro St. @ 18th St.

Not quite sure what to wear to the next big Bear mixer event? Stop in at this Castro clothing store where you can get anything from ass-less leather chaps to something resembling a Confederate Civil War uniform. Besides the fetish gear, this store also has a nice selection of western clothes, like used Levi's and Wranglers, as well as some great vintage leather jackets.

www.castrotheatre.com

The Castro Theatre was built in 1922 for $300,000, which, by today's money, would equal roughly a bazillion dollars. It is easily the most beautiful movie house in the City, and is one of the few remaining movie theatres of its era still in operation today. From its neon sign and illuminated marquee to the Wurlitzer pipe organ and art deco chandelier, words cannot convey how amazing this place looks. The icing on the cake is that the Castro Theatre only plays independent and foreign films. This place is a must see.

Market St. Railway Mural

Church St. @ 15th St.

This mural, by artist Mona Caron, is hands down one of my favorite murals in the City. It shows the history of Market Street—which in itself is the history of San Francisco—through five or six eras. It begins with the introduction of the streetcars in the 1920s and ends in an optimistically utopian future, while touching on things like the Longshoremen's strike in the 30's, Gay Pride in the 80's and 90's, and the peace marches protesting the war in Iraq. I guess it's kinda hard to really describe such a mural, so I really suggest just going down and checking it out.

Seward St. Slides

Seward & Douglas Sts.

Someone built these crazy concrete slides in the most random place in the Castro. Basically you grab a piece of cardboard at the bottom of the slides, then go up to the top, and slide down. Not exactly rocket science (at least I don't think so; I really don't know what rocket science is). My advice is to not try to hold on to the cardboard with your hands because you might scrape them. The place is a little inaccessible; you might need a car, but the way to get there is this: Take 17th Street away from the Mission, and turn left on Douglas. Then take Douglas until you hit Seward and turn right. You'll see a little park thing on your left, and that's where the slides are. Have fun!

Just like a water park, but instead of a suntan you get road-rash and a wedgie.
Photo by Dylan MacNiven.

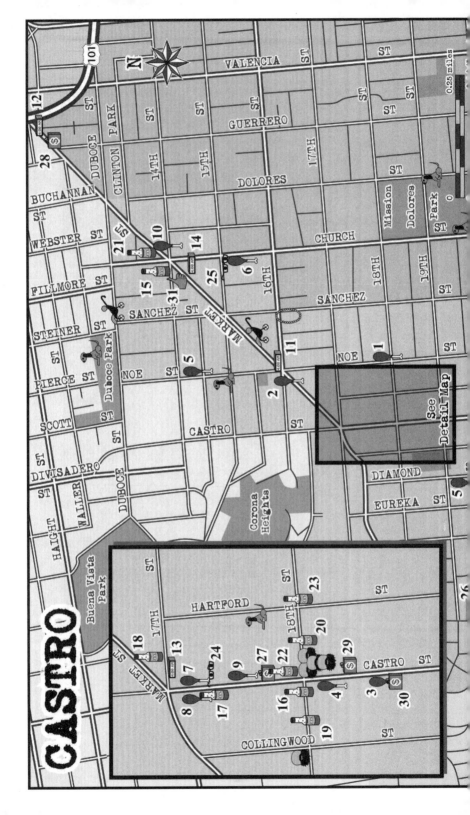

CASTRO

GRUB-A-DUB-DUB

1 7-11
2 Askew Grill
3 Castro Tarts
4 Escape From New York Pizza
5 Jumpin Java
6 No Name Sushi
7 Quickly
8 Rossi's Deli
9 Slider's Diner
10 Woodhouse Fish Company

LATE NITE EATS

11 Bagdad Cafe
12 It's Tops Coffee Shop
13 Orphan Andy's
14 Sparky's Diner

DRINKS DRINKS DRINKS

15 Amber
16 SF Badlands
17 The Bar
18 The Cafe
19 The Edge
20 Midnight Sun
21 The Mint
22 The Mix
23 Moby Dick

PLACES TO CHECI

24 Castro Theat
25 Market St. R
26 Seward St. SI

SHOPPING

27 Cliff's Vari(
28 Get Lost Tra'
29 Under One Ro
30 Worn Out Wes

Free Food!

31 Lucky 13

Buff Guys (with

Bears (Come on, wl   ?)

That one guy wh
Gras beads for s

Gay couples witl
babies

(see entry on page 226)

Happy Donuts

24th St. @ Church St.; *also* 1501 Fillmore @ Geary;
1455 Market @ Van Ness and all over the damn City

If you find yourself in Noe Valley and you're hungry and broke, then Happy Donuts is the place for you. Besides having donuts and coffee, they also make real food ranging from ham sandwiches to egg salad to hotdogs, and all for under $4. It's hard to beat that price.

Herb's Fine Foods

3991 24th St. @ Noe St.

Sticking out like a sore thumb on a neatly manicured hand, Herb's Fine Foods looks exactly like a diner should, completely anachronistic in a neighborhood like Noe Valley. I love the little horseshoe counter that allows you to make silly faces at the stranger eating across from you; and if that stranger gets even creepier than you at that moment, they have ten or so booths which allow you a little bit more privacy. The food is decent and most things cost between $5 and $7, except the steak and eggs, but I'm not one to get steak and eggs at a place where most things cost between $5 and $7.

Noe Valley Deli

4007 24th St. @ Noe St.

A family-run joint that's not much on decoration, the Noe Valley Deli is priced alright for what it is. For instance, there are a few sandwiches for $5.50. I guess the Noe Valley Deli serves its purpose, as well as Middle Eastern food.

Peasant Pies
4108 24ᵗʰ St. @ Castro St.

(see entry on page 209)

Tung Sing
4015 24ᵗʰ St. @ Noe St.

In a place like Noe Valley, where there isn't exactly a whole lot of choice in the cheap eats category, Tung Sing is a good bet. For $5.49, you can choose an item off the hot plates and it comes with a wonton and either rice or chow mein. The only thing though is that if you eat off the hot plates, they won't let you sit in the restaurant. Don't say I didn't warn you.

Sights & Entertainment

Twin Peaks Properties
4072 24ᵗʰ St. @ Castro St.

So as far as I can tell, this is just a property management place or a real estate agent, but they have my favorite window display in the City. It's a bunch of hard-line, right-wing, moderately incendiary stuff like, "I miss Reagan" signs, mixed in with photos of racehorses and old photos of the City. Hands down though, my favorite sign is the one that reads, "Welcome to Looney Valley, home of cell phones, latte-sipping liberals. This office is an island of properly conservative traditional values. A breath of fresh air for my conservative friends." Although I don't agree with the guy, I do admit he's got balls. You should really go check out his window. It's good for a laugh.

Food

Café Abir

1300 Fulton St. @ Divisadero St.

Café Abir is a really great coffee shop that also sells alcohol and always has interesting and good-looking people hanging around, studying or chatting. During the day they have a magazine store that sells both common and hard to find periodicals. The café also serves food that, although it is not as inexpensive as some places, is very tasty. Café Abir has one monumental advantage over most other coffee shops in San Francisco—from 3 to 7 p.m. every day, sangria is cheap, some beers are $2, and mini pizzas are half off.

Eddie's Café

800 Divisadero St. @ Fulton St.

Eddie's is a little diner-type place where you can get pretty good food for pretty good prices. It is not as cheap as say, Golden Coffee or Hahn's in the Tenderloin, but it is pretty damn close. You can get something like three pancakes, an egg, some bacon and toast for around $5.50. Also, the people who run it are extremely nice and had sweet soul music playing on the stereo last time I was in there.

Pizza Inferno
1800 Fillmore St. @ Sutter St.

Seemingly painted by a five-year-old on LSD, this pizza joint is
a decent place to spend your happy hour. Why? I'm so glad you
asked. From 4 to 6:30 p.m. on weekdays and 10 p.m. to closing
every night, their delicious personal pizzas are two-for-one. Also
beer here only costs $3 a pint and $12 a pitcher from noon to
6:30 p.m. on weekdays and 10 p.m. to closing, every night. Their
Thai chicken pizza is amazing but don't bother with the calzones;
they're mediocre at best.

Bars

Fly Bar
762 Divisadero St. @ Fulton St.

What first attracted me to this bar was that the word "Fly" on the
outside sign is meant to look like it's from Superfly, and since I'm
a huge Curtis Mayfield fan, I had to go in. The interior of this bar
is really nice because of its low lighting and great artwork. The
crowd can be kind of a chauncey-ass Marina crowd, but at happy
hour the bar has half-off pizzas and $3 drinks, which is a plus.
Another good thing is that you can buy 20 oz beers, but another
bad thing is that they don't serve hard alcohol. This bar is good
for a Wednesday night, because it's too crowded on the weekends.

Madrone
500 Divisadero St. @ Fell St.

Overall this isn't the cheapest spot in San Francisco; their specialty is infused vodka for fuck's sake. But on Tuesdays, this
place is a broke-ass's wet dream. Bottles of Red Stripe are $2 and
shots of Jameson are $3, plus you get to hear DJs Centipede and

Citizen Ten drop rare grooves, funk and hip-hop all night for no cover charge.

 fairly decent looking clientele. I say this because Chances, the bar that previously resided in this spot, wasn't so lucky. I think the reason it was called Chances is because, chances were, you were gonna find some ugly motherfuckers there. The reason I like this spot is because the interior looks like it could be a bar in any town. It's really a nice refuge from some of the more classy and expensive places on nearby Divisadero.

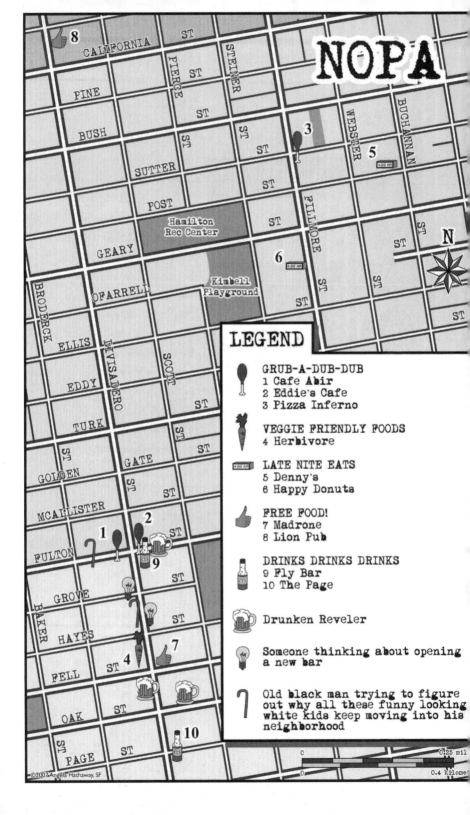

NOE VALLEY

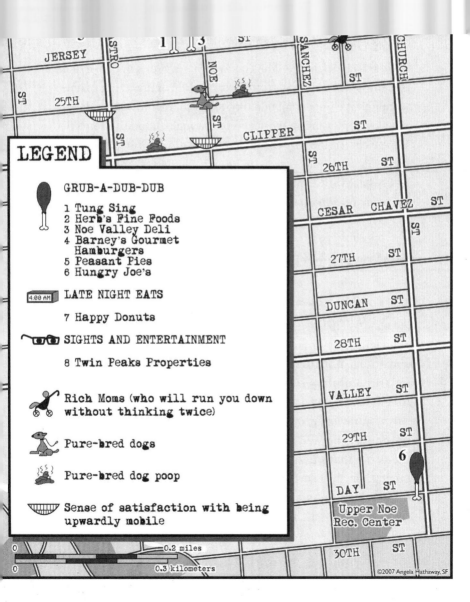

LEGEND

GRUB-A-DUB-DUB

1 Tung Sing
2 Herb's Fine Foods
3 Noe Valley Deli
4 Barney's Gourmet Hamburgers
5 Peasant Pies
6 Hungry Joe's

LATE NIGHT EATS

7 Happy Donuts

SIGHTS AND ENTERTAINMENT

8 Twin Peaks Properties

Rich Moms (who will run you down without thinking twice)

Pure-bred dogs

Pure-bred dog poop

Sense of satisfaction with being upwardly mobile

0.2 miles
0.3 kilometers

©2007 Angela Hathaway, SF

Beyond the Map

The Excelsior

The Broken Record
1166 Geneva St. @ Madrid St.

Sitting 2.5 blocks off of Mission and Geneva, this big, divey lounge
is a complete gem that's lost in the middle of fucking nowhere.
Although it can be a bit of a trek to get there, the 200 kinds of
whiskey and rotating barbecue menu make it totally worth it.
Where else in the City could you have venison, rabbit and wild
boar sausages, play pool with other delinquents, and hang out in a
lovely backyard? This is easily one of the best bars in the City, and
for some reason no one seems to know about it.

Potrero Hill

Anchor Steam Factory
1705 Mariposa St. @ Carolina St.

Delicious Anchor Steam beer has been brewed in San Francisco
since 1896. Apparently, around this time "steam" was a nickname
for West Coast beers (consider "steam" the "Hyphy" of the 1890s,
except beer instead of hip-hop), so they called it Anchor Steam.
Anyway, nowadays you can go to the factory where this amber
goodness is brewed and take a two-hour tour that ends in ... *bu
bu bu da* (that was a trumpet sound if you couldn't tell) ... a beer
tasting. Yay for beer! And the best part of this is that the whole
thing is free. But make sure to call like a month ahead of time to
make reservations. The number is (415) 893-8350.

The Presidio

1920s. I'm not sure how one goes about getting their deceased pet buried there, but it's nice to go say hello to Lady and Spot every once in awhile.

North Beach and City College

Diego Rivera Murals

In the late 1930s and early 1940s, the world famous artist, Diego Rivera (now commonly known as Frida Kahlo's husband), painted four murals in the Bay Area, two of which can be easily found in San Francisco. "The Making of a Fresco Showing the Making of a City" is in the aptly named Diego Rivera Gallery at the San Francisco Art Institute and can be seen daily between 9 a.m. and 8 p.m. The other one, "The Pan-American Unity Mural", is in the equally appropriately named Diego Rivera Theater on the main campus of San Francisco City College.

San Francisco Festivals

Here's a list of some of the festivals that go on throughout the year. Most of them are free, and the ones that require money aren't that expensive and are totally worth it. During the summertime every neighborhood has a festival, and these are a great way to have fun, drink beer on the streets and see free live music. I didn't include every free neighborhood festival because there are too many, so I included the best and most popular. Have fun.

February

Noise Pop: Going strong for more than 15 years, Noise Pop is SF's excellent, weeklong independent music festival, where bands from around the country play various venues across the city. The White Stripes, Cake, Modest Mouse and Bright Eyes are just some of the bands that have taken part in this festival over the years. The shows are not free, but definitely worth the money.

SF Independent Film Festival: This city revels in the fact that it supports independent arts. You can see some great films at this festival for good prices at cool independent theaters all over the City. Great + good + cool = too many superlatives.

Chinese New Year: Because it follows the lunar calendar, the date for this festival changes every year. It's basically all the things you expect, like firecrackers, dragons, parades and more firecrackers, but much more crowded. It takes place in Chinatown and spills out into Union Square.

Giant Pillow Fight: Every year on Valentine's Day there is a humongous pillow fight held in Justin Herman Plaza at Market and Embarcadero. Don't be a dick and put rocks in your pillow.

March

Anarchist Book Fair: I kept missing this for like four years in a row but I finally made it this year. There's all kinds of dope literature for sale, but *everything* is so political that the vibe is a little too heavy. Just because you want to tear down the American system doesn't mean vou can't have a little fun. The f...

the worst place in the world, but there is a nice parade that goes down Market Street during the daytime.

April

Alternative Press Expo (APE): If you are into zines, comic books and all things DIY, APE is a little slice of heaven. Granted there is a small cover charge, like seven bucks or so, but the concourse is filled to the brim with booths of people selling all their goods. You can get amazing things here for great prices, or (even better) people are totally down to trade their DIY stuff for yours. It's one of my favorite things that happens in the City all year long.

SF International Film Festival: Pretty self-explanatory. Films from around the world playing in theaters around San Francisco.

Ben & Jerry's Free Cone Day: Every April, Ben & Jerry's shows that they're awesome by picking a date and giving out free ice cream all day long. Just show up at one of their stores and get in line. They've been doing this since 1979. I'm sure you can just hit up their Web site to find out when it is each year.

May

Bay to Breakers: Simply put, B2B is a race from the Bay to the ocean, through San Francisco, where people dress in costumes and drink heavily. To give you a better idea of it though, I'll tell you about my experience from last year. I arrived at 9 a.m., dressed in some sort of fairy costume with an orange tutu, and met up with a group of seven intrepid companions. I cracked open my first 40 shortly afterwards. We then walked with the masses through Golden Gate Park, where we continued to drink the many free beers people gave us as well as opening and drinking our second 40s. People were passed out drunk all over the place. At the end of the park we somehow scored giant sausages for $1 each; then the heavens opened up and dumped rain on us. I began to wonder what happened to the passed out people. We ran for ten blocks before we found an Irish pub. Car Bombs were drunk, followed by vodka-and-Red Bull's. Nachos happened on Haight Street, where I was drunk enough to start delivering people's food to their tables. I somehow made it home safely and passed out at 7 p.m. I woke the next day and both my sides ached; I'm pretty sure it was my kidneys crying tears of blood; my liver was not responsive. Two weeks later I had a dream that it was B2B again and it caused me to have anxiety because it was just too early to go through that again. Bay to Breakers will fuck you up! I highly recommend it.

Cinco de Mayo: Considering the size of the Mexican population in the Mission, this really isn't as big a party as it should be. In San Jose they have riots every year. I can't believe we're getting shown up by San Jose.

Carnival: Floats, beads, sexy costumes that don't actually show nipple, and more floats. Carnival is a lot of fun in the Mission. I've actually come to the realization though that I really don't like parades. They're boring. I mean, I understand like back in the 1800s when parades were the only entertainment you got all year, but my attention span is way too short to watch hours of people and floats walking past me. The best part of the parade is when the low-riders come by and pop their hydraulics. That shit is tight! Otherwise I just go right to the fair part and buy some delicious corn on the cob. Who doesn't like fair food?

Mission Creek Festival: Another of San Francisco's fantastic independent music/art festivals, Mission Creek takes place in venues all around the City.

June

Gay Pride: Easily one of the most fun weekends in San Francisco. Saturday night is my favorite because they block off the Castro and people walk around drinking on the streets, making out, and just generally

I'm looking into your apartment window. Did you get that shower curtain at Ikea? Photo by Victoria Smith

celebrating. It's like Halloween without all the violence. Then on Sunday they do the LGBT Pride parade down Market Street that ends at a festival in the Civic Center. As I said before, I'm not a big parade fan, but who can say no to Dykes on Bikes? It's really a great weekend all around, and I especially love it because my brother comes up for it every year. He's a total homo. Actually I think I have the gayest family in the world; seriously, there are so many gay people in my family that at Passover we could have the gay table instead of the kid's table.

Union Street Festival: Old rich people and ex-frat boys/sorority girls getting wasted in the daytime and looking at booths of art and listening to live music.

Haight Ashbury Street Fair: Old hippies and younger hipsters getting wasted in the daytime and looking at booths of art and listening to live music.

Stern Grove Festival: Holding it down for over 70 years, this is the oldest free summer festival of its kind in the States. Every weekend during the summer big name acts play at this beautiful outdoor venue in the Outer Sunset. And if you're lucky, you might even see a little bit of sun ... but probably not.

North Beach Festival: All kinds of people getting wasted in the daytime, looking at booths of art and listening to live music.

SF Pro-Am League: This is a summer basketball league where professionals and amateurs make teams and then play against each other. There have been some pretty big-time participants over the years like Cliff Robinson, Jason Kidd and Gary Payton. It's free to watch the games which all happen at Kezar Stadium, just off where Haight runs into Golden Gate Park.

July

Fillmore Jazz Festival: Spanning something like 13 blocks, the Fillmore Jazz Festival is the largest free jazz fest on the West Coast. Like any outdoor free summer festival, there are tons of stages and tons of art and food vendors. Held in a historically black neighborhood, this festival celebrates the district's postwar Jazz Era heyday. I actually worked at this festival one year for Mrs. Dewson, selling her famous hats. Mrs. Dewson is a 300-pound, 60-plus-year-old black lady who I was still terrified of after she had just got back from having heart surgery. When a couple police officers asked her about her permits to sell hats on the street, she replied, "Do you know who the fuck I am? I don't have to do shit. I'll call the Mayor right now and have your ass fired and sent back to Kentucky or wherever the fuck you're from ... telling me I can't sell my hats in front of my store motherfucker." The police left her alone after that, and I soon got a new job.

North Beach Jazz Festival: A different take on jazz festivals, this one has both free shows in Washington Square Park and shows with cover charges around the City. Carlos Santana is always hanging out at the free shows in the park.

4th of July on the Waterfront: Because it is during the heart of tourist season, way too many people attend this fireworks display. But if you're into it, more power to you.

August

Stern Grove Festival: See above

SF Pro-Am League: See above

September

Folsom Street Fair: Oh yes, this is a special one. The Folsom Street Fair has to be the kinkiest street fair in the USA. Bondage, leather, naked old guys playing with themselves … this fair has it all, even public displays of whipping. You should totally take your grandmother here. Oh wait, I think I saw her last year leading your grandfather around on a leash. *Zing!*

Castro Street Fair: Compared to Pride and Halloween, this fair is pretty lackluster, but I couldn't not include it.

Power to the Peaceful: This is always a lot of fun. It's a free festival in Golden Gate Park that has tons of great live music and speakers as well as booths about how you can help save the world. Michael Franti started it in 1999 as a "Free Mumia" event, but since 9/11 it has blossomed into a festival that supports all kinds of progressive causes. Past groups and speakers who've participated include Blackalicious, Michael Franti and Spearhead, Angela Davis, Saul Williams, String Cheese Incident and Woody Harrelson. It always takes place like two weeks after Burning Man, so there's all this leftover, weird groovy energy from the desert (or maybe that just all the pot smoke). Also it's a great place to meet beautiful people … you know who you are, wink, wink.

Love Parade: I went to the Love Parade in Berlin in 2001, and it was fucking insane. There were 2 million people in the Tiergarten, in the center of the city, who were dancing, blowing each other, OD-ing, and doing just about anything else imaginable or unimaginable. I drank all day and dropped ecstasy all night. Good times. So now the Love Parade movement has spread its techno wings to other cities, including San Francisco. Although it's not nearly as big as the one in Berlin, it is still a lot of fun (and a lot more regulated, unfortunately). It's basically a big, free, daytime rave in the middle of San Francisco.

Comedy Day: What's better than hours of free comedy in Golden Gate Park? There's no punchline, I just really wanted to know.

Decompression: Taking place six weeks after Burning Man ends, Decompression is an all day party that allows Burners to do their Black Rock City thing right here in the City of San Francisco. For me to describe it more would require me trying to describe Burning Man. Go to *www.burningman.com* if you've got more questions.

October

Halloween: This used to be an amazing party where people went all out on their costumes and everyone felt free and safe to express themselves as they wished. But in recent years, more and more fuck-wads have been showing up, not dressed in costume, disrupting the vibe and causing violence. In 2006, something like ten people were shot. I know, it fucking sucks. It's definitely a spectacle to see though, because they block off the streets in the Castro and there are thousands of people milling around. But they don't even allow alcohol inside anymore. Eh, go to Pride instead. It's much safer and a lot more fun.

Hardly Strictly Bluegrass Festival: Awesome free live music in Golden Gate Park. Last year Elvis Costello, Earl

Scruggs, Billy Bragg and Emmylou Harris all played. It's really a great time.

Vegetarian/Vegan Restaurants and Stuff

Here's a list of various exclusively veggie/vegan spots around the city. I haven't actually eaten at all of them, so they're not all reviewed elsewhere in the book. Also, not all of them are cheap. But I figured I make enough references to eating buffalo and shit like that that I might as well do something for those out there not properly using their incisors. Besides, what can I say, I love you motherfuckers.

The Mission

Café Gratitude: 2400 Harrison St. @ 20th St.
Raw and organic food place with touchy-feely named dishes like, "I am sustained" and "I am terrific". They're a bit pricey but have a really neat sign.

Cha-Ya: 762 Valencia St. @ 18th St.
Veggie Japanese food.

Herbivore: 983 Valencia St. @ 21st St.
I've eaten here. The food's not bad and the servers are cute.

Little Otsu: 849 Valencia St. @ 19th St.
Cute little store that sells only vegan products like stationery and other tchotchkes.

Minako Organic Japanese Restaurant: 2154 Mission St. @ Clarion Alley
If you can't figure out what this place is about then you're fucking retarded.

Rainbow Grocery: 1745 Folsom St. @ 14th St.
Around since 1975, this fantastic grocery co-op sells all kinds of organic veggie produce and keeps it real politically. They do cool things like take part in protests and close on Cesar Chavez's birthday.

The Tenderloin

Ananda Fuara: 1298 Market St. @ Larkin St.

...ood in the City.

...gest selection

The Sunset

Daily Health Food & Deli: 1235 9ᵗʰ Ave. @ Lincoln St.
Smoothies, vitamins and hot veggie food. What more could you ask for (besides a little bit of meat)?

Enjoy Vegetarian Restaurant: 754 Kirkham St. @ 12ᵗʰ Ave.
Cute Chinese place with good fake meat, nice service and a pleasant sounding name.

Feel Real Organic Café: 4001 Judah St. @ 45ᵗʰ Ave.
This place looks exactly like you would imagine an organic cafe to look like: bright colors, plants and other general funky decorations. The only major issue is that it's closer to Japan than downtown San Francisco.

Judahlicious: 3906 Judah St. @ 44ᵗʰ Ave.
Vegan ice cream, smoothies and yummy snacks like burritos and the sherpa sandwich (apparently not made from real sherpas).

Other Avenues Food Store: 3930 Judah St. @ 44ᵗʰ Ave.
An organic, veggie, natural health food co-op/grocery store.

New Ganges Restaurant: 775 Fredrick St. @ Lincoln St.
Yummy yummy yummy Indian food. Yummy.

Shangri-La: 2026 Irving St. @ 22ⁿᵈ Ave.
There is a grip of veggie Chinese food places in the City. This is one of them.

The Richmond

Bok Choy Garden: 1820 Clement St. @ 19ᵗʰ Ave. (see page 278)
Cheap Chinese vegetarian joint laid out like an old school diner.

Layonna Vegetarian Restaurant: 1829 Clement St. @ 19ᵗʰ Ave.
Delectable dim sum with awesome fake meat dishes. How the hell did they do the fake shrimp?

North Beach

Juicy Lucy's: 703 Columbus St. @ Filbert St.
(see page 149)
Raw and organic food/smoothie place that's not exactly cheap. But come on, when have you ever seen a cheap raw-and-organic place?

Chinatown

Lucky Creation: 854 Washington St. @ Ross Alley
Small, cheap, hit or miss veggie Chinese food.

Union Square/Financial District

Medicine Eatstation: 161 Sutter St. @ Kearny St.
(in the Crocker Galleria)
Japanese food, minus the meat, at an average price. Personally, I prefer sushi.

Millennium: 580 Geary Blvd. @ Jones St.
Not even remotely inexpensive but really fucking good, this innovative vegetarian restaurants is one of the best spots in all of San Francisco.

The Marina

Alive!: 1972 Lombard St. @ Webster St.
No, this has nothing to d-

Lettus Café Organic: 3352 Steiner St. @ Chestnut St.
A trendy, average-priced spot that belongs in the Marina. It's got that sleek thing going on.

The (soon to be famous) List of Free Food

Ah, yes. The moment you've all been waiting for. You can't bullshit me, we both know this is the real reason you bought (or stole) this book. I could have filled the rest of the book with the most insightful social criticism yet written in the twenty-first century (yeah right, this is bathroom reading) and you would still have picked it up because of the (soon to be famous) List of Free Food. When you tell your friends about this book, you'll probably be like, "Yeah, that motherfucker Stuart is kinda a douche bag, but at least he gave me all these places to eat free food." I hope you enjoy filling your bellies with all these goodies, and if so, buy me drink if ever we meet. Without further ado, here we go:

The Mission

El Rio: 3158 Mission St. @ Valencia St. (see page 31)
El Rio serves free oysters on Fridays, from 5 to 7 p.m. Come on, be brave and try some.

The Last Supper Club: 1199 Valencia St. @ 23rd St.
This is a great happy hour spot because it serves tasty Italian appetizers every weekday.

The Tendernob

The White Horse Pub: 635 Sutter St. @ Taylor St.
(see page 60)
Buy a drink here on Mondays and get fed chicken wings and shit, from 5:30 p.m. until they run out.

SOMA

Eddie Rickenbacker's: 133 2nd St. @ Mission St. (see page 88)
Great variety of yummy appetizers during happy hour, Monday

through Friday. The only thing is that you've gotta wait like 30 minutes between each plate. Luckily they have a vat of gnarly cheese for you to much on.

M̶a̶—̶ ̶~̶~̶

̶~̶~̶ ̶.̶.̶o̶o̶u̶.̶

The Richmond

540 Club: 540 Clement St. @ 6th Ave. (see page 107)
Punk Rock BBQ means Sunday afternoons spent at the 540 club eating free, drinking $2 beers and listening to punk. The only thing better than that would be free barbecue, $2 beers and soul music, but I guess you can't be too picky when free barbecue is involved.

Pizza Orgasmica: 823 Clement St. @ 9th Ave. (see page 106)
Drink specials and pizza bites on Thursday nights—what a delight! No need to fight because this shit is tight. (I'm a poet and your mom fucking knows it.)

North Beach

Gino & Carlo's: 548 Green St. @ Grant St. (see page 151)
This old school joint has a free food spread on Sundays during football season.

Union Square/Financial District

Dave's Bar: 29 3rd St. @ Market St.
Okay, this one is nothing too special, but they put out shit like cheese and crackers and chips and salsa, every day. It's better than nothing.

Escape From New York Pizza: 333 Bush St. @ Montgomery St.
On the first Friday of every month, $5 gets you all you can eat

pizza and as much live poetry as you can bear.

The Holding Company: 2 Embarcadero Center (see page 177)
So-so free food Tuesday through Thursday during happy hour. But hell, it's free.

MacArthur Park: 607 Front St. @ Jackson St. (see page 178)
This place has a different food spread every weekday during HH (no, not Humbert Humbert).

Morton's Steakhouse: 400 Post St. @ Powell St. (see page 178)
Buy a drink, and get free filet mignon sandwiches. You love me, don't you?

Palio D'Asti: 640 Sacramento St. @ Montgomery St.
(see page 178)
Buy two drinks and get a free slice. The deal is kinda *meh*, but the pizza is good.

Perry's: 185 Sutter St. @ Montgomery St.
Even though the crowd here generally consists of drunk douche bags in sport coats and ties, I'll brave it for some of Perry's free chicken wings at happy hour.

Schroeder's: 240 Front St. @ Sacramento St.
On Thursdays and Fridays this spot serves free appetizers from 5 to 7 p.m. Don't miss the meatballs—they're almost better than a handjob.

The Marina

Liverpool Lil's: 2942 Lyon St. @ Lombard St.
Not a cheap place normally, but happy hour is a blessed thing. In this case that means free goodies like meatballs, mozzarella sticks and quiche. Doesn't quiche just make a place sound classy?

The Castro

Lucky 13: 2140 Market St. @ Church St. (see page 248)
Every Saturday during the summer you can show up here from 4 to 7 p.m. and get free barbecue. I think I've been here every summer Saturday for the past three years.

NOPA

Lions Pub: 2062 Divisadero St. @ Sacramento St.
There is no set schedule, but most ~~~~~~

Other

The Big Four Restaurant: 1075 California St. @ Taylor St.
(inside the Huntington Hotel)
This Nob Hill spot is a total score. It's a *super* nice restaurant that
does free gourmet appetizers during happy hour. I once sat next to
Dr. Jane Goodall, the famous chimpanzee lady, in this joint.

Sugar Lounge:
377 Hayes St. @ Gough St.
Sitting in the center of the Hayes Valley, this bar does all kinds of
delectable HH food like veggie tempura and barbecue chicken.

*There's always a point in the night when you begin
to wonder if you're drinking the bottle, or if it's
drinking you.*

Awesome and Helpful Web sites

I don't know what kind of clever things you want me to say here people. Quite simply, these are just a bunch of Web sites that, if used correctly, will greatly enhance your life in San Francisco. Consider it like *Chicken Soup for the Soul* except that these sites will probably ruin your eyesight, help you destroy your liver and maybe even assist in scoring you a case of gonorrhea.

511.org: This is a great site because it helps you navigate the city. They have a link that lets you plug in a beginning and an ending point, and then it tells you how to get there by mass transit. The only thing is that they ask way too many questions when you're planning your trip. It's like, motherfucker just tell me how to get from my house to In-N-Out—don't ask me what day I'm going. That shit is none of your business. I just want a double-double.

askascientistsf.com: This is the Web site for a super cool lecture series. Once a month, a different scientist lectures about a different topic in a different café in San Francisco. It's neat because the speakers are actually good at breaking the topics down into regular-people terms so that morons like me can understand what the fuck they're talking about. Recent topics have included amnesia and string theory. Cool, right?

craigslist.org: Whether you're looking for a job, an apartment, the cute redhead you saw on BART, a used bike or simply some no strings attached oral sex, craigslist has it all. This giant online bulletin board makes living in the City so much easier. In fact, I've found all of my apartments on this site. Craigslist is now in many major cities across the world, but it got its start right here in the City. This is one of the best resources available in the Bay Area. I once saw a post in the 'missed connections' area that said, "Last night at King Diner I was the man who puked all over the place. You were the woman who helped me clean it up. I think I love you and want to see you again. That may be fairly easy because I'm pretty sure you are a prostitute. If you want to find me I'll be the guy at 5th and Market playing chess with the brown bagged King Cobra 40." I'm not joking.

fecalface.com: I promise this isn't a sick joke

… site, you should be able to eat and drink for free most nights of the week. You love me. P.S. If you don't know what a Cleveland Steamer is, you're missing out on some serious shit.

flavorpill.net: A little bit more highbrow than some of the other sites listed in this book (just look at the names of the two sites bookending it), flavorpill.net hips you to what's going on in the worlds of art, books, music and fashion. Some of the events are not cheap, but the cheap ones are worth checking out. This site also has an email list you can sign up for.

funcheapsf.com: My man Johnny has been doing this site for a while now. It's a fucking great way to learn about dope things to do in the City that are fun and cheap. Johnny's actually responsible for hipping me to most of the stuff on my list of festivals that happen throughout the year. You can also sign up for the mailing list that not only lets you know what's happening that week, but also includes a free giveaway for random things like concert tickets or bicycles made by Paul Frank. I can't think of a single good reason for you not to sign up for the mailing list, unless you're too *cool* for mailing lists.

lilycat.com: The tagline for this site is "strange minds, strange times, things and people that purr." I'm not 100 percent sure what it means, but I like it. I also like this site. Lilycat.com is a Web site that has resources for artists of all kinds. Whether you're a musician, a filmmaker or an erotic writer, there are links on this site that can help you with what you're doing. But the real heart of the site is the event listings. Lilycat.com excels at getting the real interesting and underground shit—where else would you hear about a medical marijuana benefit, a fetish culture art show and a workshop on how to make zines?

mistersf.com: If you're interested in the people and places that make San Francisco what it is, then you're really gonna dig this site. Mister SF, aka Hank Donat, knows more about San Francisco than most of us will probably know about anything in our entire lives, and he gladly shares it with us on his Web site. Wanna know about all the famous murders that have happened in this city? Or where your street got its name? Mister SF has the 411. If you love San Francisco, you'll spend hours on this site.

myopenbar.com: Are you fucking kidding me? I can't think of a better thing in the world for broke-asses than myopenbar.com. I almost feel like these guys are my long lost brothers. Basically this site gives weekly updates on where to get free and/or really cheap drinks in SF, NY, Chicago and LA. Plus they have Seattle, Boston and DC in the works. The content is really well written and funny too. And for those of you too lazy to check the Web site, you can sign up for their mailing list and get the goods emailed to you once a week. These guys should get a Nobel Peace Prize. If you don't check this shit out, there's nothing else I can do for you; you're reading the wrong book.

onlyinsanfrancisco.com: This is the official site of the SF Convention and Visitors Bureau. It is unbelievably helpful for those of you who, like myself, are far too lazy to actually go and find the Bureau. This has all the standard info of all the basic things one might do and see in San Francisco. It's perfect for when you have out of town guests who aren't interested in watching you smoke blunts and play Grand Theft Auto all day.

sfcityguides.org: I totally like to geek out on history and architecture and shit like that. If you do too, you have to check out this Web site. San Francisco City Guides is a group that gives FREE

walking tours of SF, no strings attached. You're more than welcome to make donations though. The site has a staggering number of possible tours; this is a really done city and all but I h   i

...g ... tumultuous history of San Fran-
cisco from its beginning, way before the Gold Rush, until now. For
example they even have an archeological study called, "Unvan-
ished Story: 5,500 Years of History near 7th and Mission Streets".
Do you think 7th and Mission had as many crackheads 5,500 years
ago as it does now?

yelp.com: Think you can do this shit better than me? Go ahead
and give it a try. Yelp is a site where you can log on, write your
own reviews about almost anything from dermatologists to
Ethiopian food, and share it with other people. You can also read
everyone else's reviews and decide whether you actually want
to spend your hard earned cash on that one-armed stripper with
the eye patch. It's a fantastic site run by fantastic people, and it's
a whole lot of fun. I do have to admit that there are a few whiners
on there, but whiners are everywhere, probably including your
roommate. My only bit of advice is this: you can be honest in your
reviews without being mean. Sometimes that's the funniest shit in
the world.

Late Night Eats

San Francisco is seriously lacking in choices for late night eats. That's why I decided to put together a list to help you avoid the same two places that you go every time you want to get a bite after midnight. Enjoy, and don't forget to tip the servers well for putting up with and cleaning up after your drunk ass.

Photo by *Victoria Smith*

The Mission

El Farolito: 2777Mission St. @ 24th St. (see page 22)
This Mission staple is open until 3 a.m. on weekends. The burritos here are great, but there is a reason we call it "El Fart-a-loto".

New Yorker's Buffalo Wings: 663 Valencia St. @ 18th St. (see page 23)
Open till late on weekends, this place was awesome when the owners were Chinese and would sell us beer until 3 a.m. The new owners are Muslim, which means no beer at all … bummer. But at least you can still get wings until 3.

The TenderNob

Osha Thai Noodle: 696 Geary Blvd. @ Leavenworth St. (see page 56)
Open until 1 a.m. on weeknights and 3 a.m. on weekends, Osha is making it easy for you to get your Thai food fix as often as you want.

SOMA

Crêpes a Go-Go: 350 11th St. @ Folsom St. (see page 83)
I'm not even sure when this place closes—maybe when the last

paying customer has his or her belly full of yummy cheap crêpes.

Denny's: 816 Mission St. @ 4th St.; also 1700 Post @ Webster

Corporate......

North Beach

Broadway Express: 448 Broadway @ Kearny St.
(see page 147)
This joint serves pizza *and* burritos until 3 a.m. Are these people
gods or just geniuses? The jury is still out on that one.

Golden Boy Pizza: 542 Green St. @ Grant St. (see page 148)
Open late on weekend nights, this North Beach classic gets a huge
line once the bars let out.

Sam's: 618 Broadway @ Grant St. (see page 150)
You can't get any more real than a place that serves food that is
so-so when sober and amazing when drunk. I have never been
here sober though, so the former is just hearsay. The hours are 5
p.m. to 2 a.m.

Union Square

Café Mason: 320 Mason St. @ Geary Blvd. (see page 49)
This place is always open, which is great for many reasons. For
example, I once met a hot Canadian girl here late at night and
ended up getting her naked in a nearby hotel elevator. If that's
not a reason for a place to be open 24 hours, then I don't know
what is.

Lori's Diner: 336 Mason St. @ Geary Blvd. (see page 175)
Come to this Lori's location where the food is pretty good and it's
the 50's 24/7.

Naan 'n Curry: 336 O'Farrell St. @ Mason St. (see page 208)
This is delicious, cheap Indian food, 24 hours a day. All I need are
some Rolaids afterwards, and I'm a happy boy.

Pinecrest Diner: 401 Geary Blvd. @ Mason St. (see page 54)
The food here is not good and not cheap, but it is open 24/7.

Chinatown

Sam Wo's: 813 Washington St. @ Stockton St. (see page 193)
Sufficient tasting food at great prices and open until 3 a.m. Don't
worry, the waiters don't hate you; they're like that to everyone.

The Sunset

JT's (Island Café): 901 Taraval St. @ 19th Ave.
Diner food + Hawaiian food + really late hours = If you're in the
neighborhood, why the fuck not?

The Marina

All Star Donuts: 2095 Chestnut St. @ Steiner St. (see page 226)
Donuts, cheap sandwiches, a cool sign and it's open 24 hours.

IHOP: 2299 Lombard St. @ Pierce St.
The International House of Pancakes still exists. I totally forgot
about it. Always open, so if you're lonely on Christmas, don't kill
yourself—go to IHOP instead.

Mel's Drive-In: 2165 Lombard St. @ Steiner St.; also 3355
Geary Blvd. @ Commonwealth St.; 801 Mission St. @ 4th St.;
and 1050 Van Ness Ave. @ Geary Blvd.
I've always thought this place was a little pricey for what it was,
but it's always open late, and it's open 24 hours on Friday and Saturday. That's gotta count for something, right?

The Castro

Bagdad Café: 2295 Market St. @ 16th St. (see page 242)
Overpriced but open 24/7 with tons of greasy goodness. Too bad

it only has one bathroom.

It's Tops Coffee Shop: 1801 Market St. @ Octavia St.

Orphan Andy's: 2370 Market St. @ 17th St. (see page 244)
I've met some really strange people in the wee hours of the morning at this 24 hour spot.

Sparky's Diner: 242 Church St. @ Market St. (see page 245)
This is as hip as 24-hour restaurants get. It almost feels like anything goes here, including overpriced food.

Other

Happy Donuts: Everywhere
I feel like there is one of these in practically every neighborhood in the City. They're always open, and I'll give you one guess as to what they sell.

Lucky Penny: 2670 Geary Blvd. @ Masonic Ave. (see page 105)
Always open and always mediocre, the Lucky Penny at least serves the role as being the only late nightspot in NOPA.

Mr. Pizza Man: 1-800-570-5111
That's right, I just gave you a phone number, but do you know why? Because Mr. Pizza Man delivers at least until 4 a.m. (I know this from experience) and maybe 24 hours. Just don't be an idiot and pass out before the pizza gets there. I think you can get blackballed from their delivery list.

Polk

Bob's Donut and Pastry Shop: 1621 Polk St. @ Sacramento St.
Donuts, pastries and coffee, 24 hours a day. This place has been here forever and is somewhat of an institution. Why the hell not eat donuts at 4 a.m.? It's not like they'll make you fat.

Grubstake: 1517 Pine St. @ Polk St. (see page 51)
Open until 4 a.m. every day and serving possibly the most glorious mozzarella sticks in the universe.

Thanks

First and foremost, I'd like to thank the good folks at Falls Media for putting out this book and making it so I wouldn't have to do all this shit by myself. Next I'd like to thank all the contributors: Thanks to Victoria Smith for shooting the cover as well as other shots throughout the book; you make me look like a sexy beast. Thanks to Trisha Gum and Tobias Womack for contributing their photographic genius and helping make this the best book in Awesometown. Thanks to Angie Hathaway for being the coolest and most stylish cartographer in the world. Then there's Kenny Liu. I have no idea how you put up with me, but you manage to do it, so kudos to you, old chum. Thanks for all your amazing design work. Thanks to all my valiant proofreaders: John Armenta, Jeremy Elman, and Josh Katz. Thanks to my parents for being supportive and not being disappointed that I didn't want to grow up to be a doctor, lawyer or an accountant. Thanks to my grandparents for thinking I'm cool no matter what my current endeavors are. To my girl Krista, I love you. Thanks for loving me and letting me stay with you and for putting up with the insanity of dating someone who is trying to take over the world, one neighborhood at a time. Thanks also to Abbey and Jen for letting me stay at the house while finishing this book. Thanks to Jeremy,

Victoria Smith

Joe and JT for leaving the door unlocked all those days I needed a quiet place to work. Look under the couch, I left a stinky surprise for you. Thanks to Tia for helping support me in those lean early years, when I had no money at all and this was just a silly little zine. Thanks to all my friends for giving me ideas of places to write up and for spreading the Broke-Ass revolution by word of mouth. Thanks to anyone who ever bought me a drink or a burrito. Thanks to Tapatio salsa for making everything taste better. Thanks to all the cute girls out there who think writers are sexy. Thanks to all the stores who sold my zines and put up my posters in the windows. And most of all I would like to thank anyone who ever bought a copy of *Broke-Ass Stuart's Guide to Living Cheaply in San Francisco*, especially those of you who have been down since volume one. I love all of you! Thank you (just thought I'd throw one more in there for good luck).

Contributors

...i.... ....i.fr f-. .11 .f th. fin. folks who helped make

people's lives with custom maps infused with a splash of humor. A lot of people have no idea where they are or where they're going, so if you are looking to find yourself, this is the girl to contact. *angielovesmaps@gmail.com*

Cover design: Kenny Liu does not believe in right angles and he would like nothing more than to draw you a pretty picture. He has also been given the key to the city of Des Moines, Iowa. He has yet to use it. *structives.com*

Cover photo as well as other photos: Victoria Smith is a queen, a rebel, a renegade, a lover of life and wannabe-er of good will. Her photos are some of the best in the world and you should employ her as much as possible so she may continue to light up her own life, as well as the saps around her. Seriously though, this shit don't stink. *www.VictoriaSmithPhoto.com, mamavic22@yahoo.com*

Interior Design: Mike Force is an illustrator and designer living in Brooklyn. *www.mikeforce.org, mikeforceillustration@gmail.com*

Photos: Trisha Gum is a multimedia artist and filmmaker. Trisha has lent her talents to creating band posters for the famous Fillmore Auditorium and has maintained success as a band and commercial photographer. Trisha currently resides in Los Angeles where she is working on her film career and as a fine artist. *www.tgumphoto.com, tgumphoto@hotmail.com*

Photos: Tobias Womack is a maverick and a madman. *www.tobiaswomack.com*

Alright, it's your turn. I've done enough babbling about free food, cheap drinks and beautiful neon signs, so I'm handing it over to you. I left some room here at the back of the book so you can take notes about your own adventures (or mishaps) in this strange city. Write about your favorite restaurants, bars, shopping, sights & entertainment, or just use it to write down the phone number of the cute brunette at the end of the bar. Or do nothing with it. I don't really care, but it's here if you want it.

Food

Shopping

YOU ARE YOUNG. BROKE,

The book you're holding is just the beginning of what I've got for you; it's just the sore that signifies the sickness. You want more? Come visit me online for a whole bunch of other cool shit like:

- Broke-Ass Stuart updates
- New entries and forums
- Day-to-day thoughts and adventures
- Travel blogs and photography
- Videos, pictures and other media
- An online store
- And even a motherfucking advice column (yup, I might get arrested for that one)

One more thing...

There is so much to see, eat, and drink in San Francisco that it was impossible for me to get every single good deal into this book. Therefore, I would like to ask all of you a favor: if you come across something in the City that you think would be great for the next edition of this book, please drop me a line at www.brokeassstuart.com. Also, if you have any praise, criticism, love letters or death threats you wish to send me, please feel free to send them as well.

Thanks a lot.

Broke-Ass Stuart

BRoKe-ASS StuART